Ball Four, Take Your Base!

Baseball at San Quentin Prison: The 2011 and 2012 Seasons

Kent Philpott

EVM

Ball Four, Take Your Base!
Baseball at San Quentin: The 2011 and 2012 Seasons

Copyright © 2025 Kent Philpott

Earthen Vessel Media, LLC
San Rafael, CA

ISBN (print): 978-0-9968590-9-7

Library of Congress Control Number: 2025921808

All rights reserved. Photographs and stories used by permission. Photographers: Katie L. C. Philpott, Bill Mauck, Scott Ostler

Interior and Cover Design: Katie L. C. Philpott

No Part of this publication may be reproduced, stored in a retrieval system, or transmitted in any form or by any means, electronic or mechanical, including photocopying, recording, or by any information retrieval system, without the written permission of the author or pubisher, except by a reviewer who wishes to quote brief passages in connection with a review written for inclusion in a magazine, newspaper, internet site, or broadcast.

Contents

Early Troubles	5
The Memo	8
The Quarantine	9
Setting the Rosters	12
The Death Letter	15
Just When I Thought It Was All Good	17
Insight and Remorse	19
Opening Day	21
Sanity vs. Insanity	25
First Loss	27
Two Outs, Nobody On...	29
All About Respect	32
Johnny and Curtis	34
It Was a Tsunami	37
The Con?	40
Softball Swing	42
Full Blast Rivalry	44
Convict Mentality	46
Our Captains Have Fallen	49
Bullies	51
One in the Face	53
Curtis and the Justice	55
Over Familiarity	57
Rage, Anger, and Hate	59

The Coaches' Speeches	61
San Quentin	66
Baseball	66
Photos	66
2012 Preface	80
2012 Introduction	83
More Death Threats	86
First Day of Tryouts	89
Opening Day	91
Scheduling	93
Thin Ice	96
Suspended	98
Barred from the Prison	100
Just Before the End	104
Letter of Resignation	105
Back In: Six Years Later	108
Bill's Story	112
Doug's Story	115

1
Early Troubles

A memo announcing Tryouts for the baseball teams was posted well in advance of Saturday, February 26. Fifty-plus convicts came to try out, and the coaches were all present, armed with clip boards and pens. After warm-ups, throwing, and some running, we started the basic rotation drill to watch the guys field grounders, throw, and catch. Then we gathered names for those who wanted to try out, noting their housing, release date, and desired position.

Right away it became clear we had a problem: a little more than half of the guys who were trying out said they would be playing for the A's. That meant they were not intending to play for the Giants, the team of which I was head coach.

The idea for a second team called the A's emerged late last season. Originally there was supposed to be an intramural prison league developed, but it morphed, due to my weakness and desire to please, into something more. Basically, the intramural team started bragging they were better than the Giants. For some reason I allowed the two teams to play each other and even brought in two outside teams for the second team to play. Now I am paying for it.

After a series of meetings with convicts and prison staff, I agreed to run two teams for 2011. There was not enough of the old Pirates uniforms to make it work, so I wrote a letter to the major league Oakland A's and they were gracious enough to provide a full set of really nice uniforms. This is how the second team became the A's.

The volunteer "beige"[1] card holder who was to oversee the second group allowed the inmates to run the entirety of the operation. He did that

---

1   Prior to 2011 the ID card for volunteers who had earned the right to enter and move about the prison without an escort to conduct whatever it was they were doing was called a "brown card." That was due to the card's brown border. For some reason brown went to beige, so we are stuck with "beige card."

well enough, but he had no real say in the process, including making out the lineup and other duties always assumed by the team manager.

In time, I woke up to the problem and brought in two old friends, Ed and Ollie, to manage the A's team with the other coach still working with the players. It seemed like a solution.

On the first day of tryouts my solution fizzled. The inmates were in charge.[2] Even Steve, Ed, and Ollie, the guys who were to run the B team, were left out, though I tried to intervene. One particular inmate, a youngish white guy named Bobby, a good ball player, had taken control of the team. I mean solid control. He had it all mapped out, planned out, and that would be it. He had already determined who would be playing for the A's, so the tryouts were a farce.

One of my concerns was that the team is mostly white with one black—a necessity, since he is the only actual starting pitcher. Looks a little like the Aryan Brotherhood with a token black thrown in for appearance sake. That may not be entirely accurate, but the thought went through my mind.

The de-facto manager, Bobby, also had plans to start an intramural league on top of it all, which he announced to me, though he knew I am supposed to be in charge of the baseball program. Actually, this man is now in charge of the second team, and I will have to do something to alter what he already has in place. The B team coaches, due to no fault of their own, will either not survive the situation or will more likely refuse to be a part of it. These men are real baseball guys who have years of experience running baseball clubs.

With Ed and Ollie out, or marginalized at best, Steve will merely watch the proceedings and allow the inmates to run the A's. Already there is pressure on me to allow them to have the same status as the Giants in terms of practice time and schedule. I have a decision to make. My gut tells me to withdraw now. It is nothing but a collision about to happen. If I give in, the program could easily end. The A's, lacking strong leadership, will deteriorate into an arguing bunch of cons.

Sure, someone else could run the program, and I would hate to give it up much less have it taken from me. I enjoy the whole thing; it is real baseball, and I am fascinated with developing the system. But I resent being pushed around, maybe out, by the convicts.

Bobby informed me that those state employees in charge of educa-

---

2   Volunteers have only so much authority, and we depend on the cooperation of the inmates. Without that, nothing much happens.

tion/recreation are behind him. Indeed, I found that the usual convict manipulation had been under way. This sort of thing is a constant in prison. It is often called making a "duck" out of someone. It usually begins with flattery, working hard to help a staffer, favorably comparing the person with others, then slowly, and ever so carefully asking for a favor. Granting the favor is a violation of the state's operating manual and could also be a crime, and once committed, things are headed down a very slippery and dangerous slope. It is easy to adopt the inmate's world view and begin to both sympathize and empathize with them. Once that is done, the inmates have a duck.

Every year it is strife and anxiety for me. Why do I subject myself to it? Is it the adrenaline rush I get from being at the prison—which I do think I experience. Maybe it is the little bit of media attention that comes my way? Do I pride myself on my longevity as baseball coach at San Quentin? Maybe I just like being called "coach," which is what one player told me was why I came in year after year. Could be some of all of these. Who cares? I do it and that is about it. So another year looms full of the usual potential for constant conflict and unnecessary stress, which go together to produce an unsafe environment for me physically and emotionally.

2
The Memo

The memo reads:

Our coaches are in agreement—to begin again with the team selection process.

Either of the following approaches is acceptable for the 2011 season.

1. Work off the present arrangement with the players for the Giants to be selected by the Giant's coaches, and to disregard the players selected for the A's team which was done by the inmates, and the A's coaches select the players for that team.

OR

2. Have a draft wherein all the potential players are put into a pool and the coaches select the teams, 17 players for each team plus 3 inmate coaches.

This last concept we intend to put into place for 2012, the draft from a pool of players where the coaches select the players.

Our consensus is that under the present situation where the inmates are allowed to determine the makeup of the team—this is unacceptable and undermines the entire coaching concept.

From my perspective, and to prevent more grumbling, the first option might be better. I am, however, willing to go with either. My concern is twofold: one, preserve the fine coaching staff we have in place right now. Two, avoid situations that might jeopardize the sports program in toto. As I observe things, with twenty-nine years at the prison and sixteen as the baseball coach, we have a potential disaster on our hands with the inmates in charge. Some of them may respond that they have their coach, but it is a coach who deliberately lets the inmates run the program. This is dangerous, especially if this particular coach is allowed to set his own agenda and begin bringing in his own teams and cross scheduling games.

Kent Philpott
March 1, 2011

3

The Quarantine

March 19, 2011

A quarantine due to an outbreak of chicken pox in North Block has wiped out the practices until the 28th of March. On March 5th the quarantine went into effect. The Giants had gotten the roster down to 19 players, meaning two more needed to be cut. The A's tryout day was cancelled, which had been the 5th, but they mostly know who will be on the team anyway.

Funny how the state built a multi-million dollar hospital, which overlooks the baseball field, but those sick with the chicken pox were not moved into it. Instead, the sick convicts were left in the block to infect others. I mean, talk about close quarters. Naturally, the disease spread to more inmates until the quarantine was extended to April 16, or beyond, who knows, so we moved opening day to May 7. Of course, the guys cannot practice or exercise at all. Our pitchers, who had been throwing regularly and getting in baseball shape, will have to start over, somehow, and in their tiny, cramped cells.

I have not scheduled any April games for the A's, since I am not completely satisfied it will come off yet.[1] But, my memo worked.[2] The educational/recreational staff had no difficulty in backing me and the program we were hoping for. Steve, who was that coach I had been talking about, the one who allowed the inmates to run the team, and I are okay now but with some issues undecided. We are waiting now to see if Bobby and the others will actually yield control of the team. Convicts simply should not run the team,

---

1	Nearly all the Giants schedule is set now except for five games in August. Since outside teams know the A's are the "B" team, it is proving difficult to fill up their twenty game schedule. But it will happen, because there will be teams who will badly want to come in even if they have to play the B team.

2	The memo's success was short lived, as the whole mess had to be dragged once again into meetings with the education/recreaction brass. By opening day, May 7, many key issues remain unresolved.

though they had been able to do a fairly good job of it. Last year's intramural team that morphed into the B team was run by the cons. I have done what I could to provide that Ed, Ollie, and Steve take charge, but it remains to be seen.

As mentioned previously, the A's guys hate the idea of being a B team, but they are. The top players are Giants. A new guy, Frank—young, lefty, throws hard and is accomplished. He arrived at the prison just days before the tryouts, and both teams wanted him. After some considerable politicking, he went with the Giants. Now we will have four good starters—Kevin Driscoll, who I want to pitch on opening day, Matt White, Frank Braby, a potential real phenom, and Mario Ellis. Frank also plays center and looks great at the plate, so we have to have his bat in all the time.

I had to inform Chris Marshall, last year's center fielder, that we would ask him to move to left field. He really didn't like it and let me know it. Later he came back and said he would do it if it would help the team.

Chris comes from a rock solid family in Long Beach. He talks about his parents a great deal. He feels so bad that he has let the family down, being the black sheep as he calls himself, and he is Black. Drugs got the better of him twice, since this is the second time he has been in prison. He plays hard and is quite emotional. He gets on himself a bit too much, if he makes an error. One thing I know is that Chris has my back in the prison, and he is nobody to fool with.

Some of the guys are getting older and slower. James at 2nd, Red at 1st, Duck in left last year, Bilal in right last year. Younger guys are waiting to take their places. I can see the anxiety in their faces, the uncertainty. Terry Burton, a bench player mostly the last few years, is moving into his mid-fifties, with the grey hair appearing more obvious now. While he may be the smartest player on the team in a long while, has opted to play for the A's where he figures he will get more playing time. We talked about it and I supported his decision.

We miss Chris Rich, now in the Duelle Institute, or DVI, in Tracey, CA. I have approval now to visit him, and I hope to do so soon. Johnny, last year's team captain and our catcher, is ready again. He is counted as Hispanic, but he lacks any of the physical characteristics of that ethnic group. He has the tattoos, speech, and body language of the proto-typical convict. I have found him to be a reliable man, one I can depend on. When I need information, and so on, I go to Johnny to talk. He has the best interests of the program at heart and gets the job done.

Johnny is a lifer. I never asked him what his crime was, and he never volunteered it either. Chris Rich, whom I consider a friend even though volunteers are not supposed to develop such "familiarity" with a convict, was always the guy I could depend on to talk real with and receive accurate information about the state of things with the players. Now it is Johnny, and he is easy to reach, since he works in the garden area with Frankie, our first base coach, just inside the main entrance to the prison. We have had a number of conversations in that spot, with Johnny leaning on a rake or a shovel.

No wooden bats this year—they have splintered into what looks like weapon stock, so only metal this year, none of which can be kept in the prison. The coaches have to bring in the bats and only three. Inventory control is tight now, and there is another new warden who will want to make it look like he is doing the job, so more rules are likely on the way.

The racial makeup this year is a little less Black, little more white, and enough players housed in North Block, so that if H Unit gets locked down we can still play a game.

At least as it appears right now, there are no real troubled guys on the Giants team for 2011. Bad chemistry on the bench is the worst to overcome, and this year I am committed to dealing with it at once.

We could have a sixty-game schedule, forty for the Giants and twenty for the A's. I wanted to prevent any of the baseball players from playing on the softball team, but the A's players, those likely to make that team, protested strongly, since they are also the softball players. I relented but then halved their schedule. In the long run, both teams would play approximately the same number of games, and with 25% fewer teams to bring in, my load would be lighter. I was afraid of the reaction, however, when I let this out during the second day of the tryouts. Strangely, I did not get any static about it. We will see, but I have got the scheduling locked down under my authority, and it would be virtually impossible to alter that.

It was necessary to ordered 20 A's caps, belts, and socks from T & B Sports in San Rafael owned by the Brusati brothers, Jeff and Mike. They give me a good discount. The Oakland A's gave us uniforms, jerseys and pants, really nice stuff, big league stuff, but we needed to supply the rest of the uniform. We want our guys looking sharp.

And the Giants have new stuff, too. Mike Murphy, long time equipment manager for the San Francisco World Champion Giants, sent a bunch of stuff over, which I have yet to see. Mainly I need baseballs. Without the Giants giving us their used game balls, the whole program would not be played the same way it is now.

Here we are, a big time prison, San Quentin, real convicts, who need to be there and safely locked up, wearing the most expensive big league uniforms, running around on the nice green grass, playing a game and getting a lot of attention for it as well. All at no cost to the tax payer, I might add.

Right or wrong? Good or bad? Fair or foul? I don't deal with these questions anymore. I just do it.

4
Setting the Rosters

The Giants roster is mostly for the veterans returned from 2010, except for Terry Burton, who thought he might not make the team so went with the A's.

Terry is very helpful for both teams in terms of helping with the field, the equipment, and gathering the information needed to create the memos allowing the players to be released early for practice and games.[1] In his early fifties now, he can still play the game, pitch, play first, and any outfield position. While playing right field I have seen him throw out more than one man who thought his hit to right meant a single. We are friends, and we treat each other with respect.

There are a couple of new guys on the team, and one is Frank Braby. Tall left hander, young, red headed, played college ball in the South Bay, and a real pitcher. He must throw in the low-to-mid 80s and is a real vacuum in center. He will be perhaps our best hitter and fastest runner, faster than Mike Tyler or Charles Lyons. He's quiet and unassuming, and it's not clear what brought him to prison, but he is in H Unit so not a lifer. Probably something to do with dope, possession, dealing, something like that, but no violence or sex-related crime, I think.

Matt White is back pitching, at third base, with a good swing—well instructed, obviously having played a lot of baseball. He disappeared midway in the 2010 season: he wanted to go back to court and get any outstanding issues taken care of. He had been due to be released around September of 2010, but as a result of facing up to legal troubles, he will be with us for at least the whole of the 2011 season. Matt must be in his late thirties, and has

---

1   A change from 2010, the players will no longer be released early as always in years past. Perhaps this is the influence of the new warden, but probably comes from the new captain overseeing North Block. It means that the players are not ready to come down to the lower yard until 5:30pm, and thus our games will not begin until about 6:30pm. Games must stop at 7:45pm—maybe allowing for 4 innings.

lost about twenty pounds and looks to be in good shape. I'm not sure who will be the ace of the team—he, Frank, Kevin, or Mario. Four starters—one could have a worse problem! One or maybe two will have to pitch in relief. I'd love to have a Brian Wilson type closer.

Our coaching staff is back in tact—Kevin, Elliot, Mike, and of course, Stan, and Stan is no coach. He is the enforcer, the guy who settles problems and cuts the hard deals. In his mid-to-late 70s now, Stan was a cop for 25 years in San Francisco and ran security for Bill Graham Presents, the rock and roll impresario, for another 15 years. Stan roams the lower yard, talking to cons, and getting the job done. He often asks me if there are any problems needing to be taken care of. I tell him, and done. I don't know how he does it; he has no power and no authority except moral authority.

Stan and I met at a gym in San Rafael at least twenty years ago and became good friends. He has worked on my little television show, The Bible Study, for more than twenty years now. It is not an exaggeration when I say I would never have lasted at the prison all these years without Stan looking out for me.

Our inmate coaches are Frankie Smith, Douglas (have not learned his last name yet), and Curtis Roberts. Curtis, a three striker, all non-violent crimes, wants to focus on cleaning up the goose crap before games and practices. Geese, great big fat geese, Canadian geese, make the outfield a real mine field. It is illegal to chase them or molest them in any way. Years ago I heard a story about an Asian convict who grabbed one, wrung its neck, stuffed it inside his prison issue blue coat, then defeathered it, cleaned it, and fried it in a container of oil of some kind. Story is it took him months to build the cooker, collect the oil, and figure out a way to run a wire from his cells light socket to the cooker—and presto, cooked goose. Sadly, as I understand it, he never got a bite down, since the smell of the cooking goose wafted down to the cops at the desk in North Block. I think a three month stretch in the hole was all the reward he got. Whenever I see those damned geese crapping all over our field I think of that guy who only wanted to taste something good he had made. I would have rewarded him for ingenuity if nothing else.

The A's, now run by Ed, Ollie, and Steve, looks to be a good team, a B team, but a good team. We are going to start and end our season playing the A's. The tension is already building, and yesterday evening we had an intense scrimmage. I umpired from behind the pitcher's mound, and I had to be very careful with my calls.

The A's, the rebels or the no name team of last year, have earned respect from the way they have approached the situation this year. The cancer types are quiet, and the big troublemaker has been cut, and I did not need to have a thing to do with it. The bottom line is that the guys just want to play baseball, and they felt they had to muscle me to get it done. And the way I acted last year only fed their concerns. Now it appears that we are going to be able to cooperate and enjoy some baseball. Who knows what will happen down the road.

Kevin and I settled on seventeen players per team with three inmate coaches per team. That means I have to bring in twenty Giants and A's uniforms, plus all the rest of the equipment. Baseball is not a cheap sport to operate at all anymore. When I was a kid growing up in Los Angeles not much money was involved. Not so now. To play the game with all the right stuff—jersey, pants, cleats, gloves, socks, belts, undershirts, and caps, you are looking at around $250 per player. Then bats, catcher's gear, batting helmets, and baseballs—around another $500. Baseballs—we will go through $180 worth a week. Two teams, three games a week require a dozen balls per game, and a dozen balls will cost $60. Maybe a little less if we are able to retrieve the balls that go over the wall into industry, but over the course of sixteen weeks several thousand dollars' worth of baseballs will be needed. There are other costs as well: batting gloves, cups, and jock straps (the guys do hope they will one day get out), and other stuff that goes with the game like donuts for the bats, pine tar, even a resin bag for the pitcher. It goes on. What transpires is that the coaches "find" much of this stuff, with outside teams helping out in various ways that cannot be discussed here.

Bobby, the player who lobbied for a second team really hard last year, boasted he was going to start another team, and was in a sense squaring off against me, is still very much a presence, but we have learned to get along and a little more—not exactly friends but cooperative colleagues. He revealed that he has been in prison for fourteen years and is only thirty-two years old. He has at least eleven more years to do. A lifer, we say—the felony murder rule, and he was not the shooter. Not sure of all the details, but I would guess the usual: dope, gang, young, stupid, stoned, and wanting to show he was a tough guy. In a moment life changes and irreversibly. An old story.

5
The Death Letter

A "kite" is the usual description of a note found that bears a warning to someone in particular. I am not sure why the term "death letter" was used instead of kite. Hope I don't find out.

I heard about it as soon as I hit the lower yard for the Giants' practice Thursday night, April 21. The letter had been "sent" from an A's player to a Giants player, or so it was said. Serious stuff, and if knowledge of the letter found its way into the hands of prison officials, that would likely be the end of baseball at San Quentin. Imagine an attack, whether successful or not, on a player from another player—it could easily make headlines.

The letter was directed at a Black Giants player; it was found on the floor in PIA—prison industries where a lot of the convicts work. No one knows who sent it. Word is that the author was an A's player. If the writer was a white player, and there are only two black players on the A's, neither of which would I ever suspect of doing such a thing, then we have a racial situation on top of it all, one that could spill over into the general population. Somebody could get killed.

The player who had received the death letter approached me shortly after I reached the dugout. He was moving quickly, stuck out his hand to me, quietly told me he could not come to practice and was gone in an instant. No conversation; I merely whispered "I understand."

It was at this point that for the third time while at the prison that I was accused of being a racist. And this directly from an A's player. It was openly stated and prompted a meeting with the acting head of education. I guess the charge would really have to be reverse racism, since at least half of the Giants are Black while the A's are almost completely white. I may have inadvertently earned the derogatory designation when, after reviewing the A's roster, I commented that the A's looked like the Aryan Brotherhood Baseball Team. That was a mistake on my part.

Not sure now where to go with this. Maybe it will go away. Maybe the players will take care of it themselves. One thing is clear—I will have to be paying close attention.

Perhaps it is unrelated, but I had to have a player on the A's removed from the field sometime after the death letter incident came to my attention. He is one of the poison types from last year whom the coaches did not want on the Giants. Now an A's player, he cannot accept that his team is the "B" team. And I understand that, since I managed the B team twice in my tenure at the prison. It was of my own choosing, but being the second, not as good team, carried with it a kind of stigma. Ego-wise, you want to be on the A team on opening day; yes, I understood that it was enough to be a convicted felon locked up for pretty close to life without also being on the B team.

To come back with, "Well, it is a privilege to play baseball at all while you are in prison for murder" is true enough, but pride and self-esteem are at stake, and convicts will struggle mightily to find some for themselves.

The man was escorted off the yard with a few hundred convicts watching. And everyone knew, or would know, that I had requested it. It is a rare and unusual thing to do, and I have done it only one other time which was to prevent a fight from breaking out between two players during a practice session. The convict would either be proud or embarrassed at being led back to his cell; I learned later he was embarrassed.

Death letter: might I be the subject of one of these, or worse yet, no warning at all? How deep will feelings go? Some convicts with long sentences lose hope, and spending the rest of their lives cut off from the general prison population is not much of a deterrent. Desperation and blind rage—these are not uncommon emotions in a prison. Something other than brotherly love has been driving this particular man ever since I have known him. How desperate and angry is he, and I would be the perfect target. Everybody has got to have someone to blame, someone to hang the dark feelings on, someone to sic the demons on. Hate and rage find outlets on inanimate and not even symbolic objects. I had better stop thinking about it.

6

Just When I Thought It Was All Good

Three days before opening day, which is May 7, I am licking my wounds from being pummeled at yet another meeting with the supervisors, whose names I cannot mention due to political and other reasons.

It was bad. The cons had gotten their way, it seemed, and all my plans were set aside—the number of games the A's would play, who would schedule the games for them (not me), and the "B" status of the team. I was blindsided and things were said about me, supposedly by my own coaches, which put my reputation at risk.

For a day after the meeting I did nothing. Next I polled my coaches to see if anyone had actually complained about me. It took an hour to find out there was nothing to the accusation at all. I knew it was a phony charge, but I had to be able to state clearly and emphatically what had taken place. We reasoned that it had to come from one certain state employee who resented the authority I had. Perhaps so, but now there was turmoil among the coaches, since the employee had gotten two of them to undertake the responsibilities I have exercised for years.

Upon finding out what had happened behind closed doors ,I merely relented and said okay. After two days, however, everything went back to normal. When faced with it, and especially by the way they had been manipulated into areas they did not want to go, my coaches refused to go along, and now we are in union with each other again.

My son Vernon had been to the meeting as well. Though this is only his second year at the prison—he runs the flag football program—he made a statement that was spot on. He talked about how the inmates will try to get one person against another, divide and create divisions. Vern warned that once that occurs, the sports programs are in jeopardy.

I am not perfect. Though I try to fairly exercise the power and authority that has accrued to me over the years, I will sometimes go too far. I know it when I am doing it.

The inmates are used to being abused, and I very much do not want to be abusive. It can happen all too easily, and I have been guilty here. I become protective of what I have developed and struggled for. My rationale always is, "I am protecting the program." A time or two I have lost my temper and yelled at a player, which will weigh on my conscience for weeks or longer. Sometimes I will chalk up my character defects to the stress and strain we are all experiencing in the prison. I am the anxious type, anyway, and being at SQ is not a relaxing, pleasant event. Most of the time I am wary of cons running on either me or someone I am responsible for. Wish it were not so, but some of the convicts' claims against me are legitimate. When I become aware of them, I try to learn and change. Frankly, I am not so good at this.

I am not sure yet, but this may be my last year at the prison. How long can I do it physically? My frustration flash point seems to be reached more quickly now. I do not want to abuse the inmates more than they already have been and for many, for all of their lives. Sympathy and empathy have their place in human relations, but if taken too far these qualities can become problematic. Striking a balance requires wisdom born of experience.

7
Insight and Remorse

The California board of prison terms—the people who grant parole dates—like to estimate whether a convict have reached some form of insight into their crime and are remorseful for it as well. Insight and remorse—the road to freedom. Insight: I think this must involve whether or not a criminal understands that he or she has broken a law and that punishment must follow.

Hard core career type criminals, the socio- or psychopaths among us, apparently have little or no conscience and break laws and hurt people with little or no concern. All that counts is the satisfying of needs and desires. This is likely accurate to some degree. The trouble is that the real pro, the hardened crook, is an excellent liar and persuader. I know, since I have fallen victim more than once. These folks are charmers, highly skilled at deception, and are devious almost beyond detection.

The career criminal recognizes only two types of people: civilians and people like themselves. Civilians like me are to be taken advantage of, used. We are the suckers who have stupidly accumulated possessions that can be, ought to be, appropriated. How is it that such a person has anything approaching genuine insight? It can only be feigned.

Cons have their informal schools on how to beat parole boards. They know what the panels want to hear: stock phrases are "I broke the law, I did the wrong thing, and I am sorry for it." The lies are well rehearsed.

But there might be actual remorse. In Shawshank Redemption, Morgan Freeman's character, Red, tells a parole board, "I think about my crime every day." He is granted parole, and rightfully so. Was he having genuine remorse?

Most felons are remorseful; they have remorse over having lost their freedom, being away from their families, being stuck with people like themselves (who are not the best company), and a host of other easily understood reasons. How remorse is measured is probably impossible to say. Who could judge such a thing? Maybe remorse is triggered by breaking the law, even taking something from someone that you had no right to, like a life. Is it something that is felt or understood? How about a combination of the two?

Parole boards hear words, observe body language, spot something in the look on a face—arbitrary at best, and the prize often goes to the best actor. Perhaps there are actions, achievements, objective statistics, or anonymous evaluations from others, something that might take the pressure off both convict and parole board member. Insight and remorse—who but God could possibly know?

8
Opening Day

There was some doubt whether the opening day game would be played on May 7. There was the kite dropped about Chris Marshall, the racist charge, the missing jersey, and the battle over the status of the A's—were they an A team or a B team. If the prison got word of the kite, or death threat letter, supposedly from an A's player, maybe a white player, as Chris is black—the 2011 baseball season would likely be lost. We managed to keep it a secret known only to about two thousand inmates.

Racism—in my case it would be reverse racism, was clearly absurd, and no one entertained it for long. The whole of it seems to me to be nothing more than an attempt to sabotage the season. Perhaps a jealous wannbe ball player, or maybe just an angry man who can't stand others enjoying themselves and who sat up long nights figuring how to cause mischief. It will probably remain a mystery.

May 7, 2011, 8:30am, we were at the East Gate, and there were a number of us. In my van were Jim Parker, Vern Smith, and Shane Hedegar along with the video cameras and tri-pods. My intent was to document the event. And Bill Mauck, my old friend, was sitting in the front passenger seat with his camera to take photos as he has done for a number of opening days. I have thought it might be possible to produce a documentary, and suspecting this might be my last chance to do so, I had plotted carefully during the run-up to the game to have all the pieces in place. With no storyline in mind, I considered that it might be little more than a keep-sake, or something to show family and friends, but nevertheless, I wanted to document opening day.

Lt. Sam Robinson, the prison's public information officer and an A's fan, would be there to assure that cameras could be taken into the prison. No Lt. Robinson, no cameras; this would also be a chance to take team photos as well as individual shots. Many of these photos I will put up on Flickr, so families and friends of the guys can view them. This is not a small deal, and the guys will press me to get it done. As soon as they know the photos are up, they will get the word out.

It was the usual confusion on the lower yard with the hustle to get the uniforms on, the field prepared and striped, and a whole lot of other details attended to.

The A's were throwing out in right field. They occupied the first base dugout, the dugout used by the visiting team. A couple of weeks ago one of them, sent by the "brain trust" of the A's, approached me and asked if there would be a coin toss to see which team would be the home team. My answer was one word, "No!".

The Giant's were stretching in left field. I walked out to check on the emotional condition of the guys; the desire to beat the A's and just smash them, prove to them they were not an A team was running higher than I hoped. I knew it would surface, and I had not done a good job in cooling things down. The whole team knew I wanted to win, and badly. We all suspected that if the A's won, they would be demanding to be the A team, and that would be utterly intolerable. The stakes were indeed high. Stakes—a lot of betting would be going on, too.

Now I was also anxious. For the A's, Marvin Andrew was going to be the starting pitcher, Ke Lam would be at short and batting leadoff—anything can happen in a one game series.

Kevin Loughlin and I had figured out a line-up two days earlier, at the Thursday night practice, and before we left that night I read it out to the guys. This has long been a practice of mine, so the players could mentally and emotionally adjust to their assignments whether as a player on the field or on the bench.

A couple of players would be disappointed, too, Marcus Crumb for one. As our back-up catcher, he was no Johnny Taylor but has improved considerably since last year. Stafont Smith, the third base back-up to Matt White and Kevin Discoll, third on the depth chart; I thought he might be expecting to start. Stafont is a very good player but not to the caliber of Matt and Kevin. If I were him, I would switch to second base which would mean that only James Bautista would be in front of him. Pete Steele would feel bad, but he was behind Redd Casey at first base, so he knew he would not be a starter.

Pete Steele played for me before. Probably about 2001 he was on the team and pitched. It was a real fluke how he came to be on the team. Early that year we had a Wednesday night game, and the Hispanics were locked down in North Block, and the whole of H Unit was also locked down. I don't recall why but probably fighting, racial stuff, Mexicans versus blacks. Only seven players showed up to play, and by the same time I found out about the trouble, I saw the visiting team walking down cardiac hill toward the ball field. In desperation I walked over to the fence behind the Giant's dugout and yelled out, "Anybody know how to play baseball?"

Two cons walked up to me and said they could play the game and would play ball right then. Pete was one of them. He pitched that game, warmed up a little, and ended up winning the game and playing for the team the rest of the year. The other walk-on was Donnie Worthy, a Black guy, and he caught Pete that game and became our starting catcher the rest of the year. Donnie was voted MVP for the season. I will never forget it, and now Pete and I talk about that season and team since he is back.

The game was not all that interesting, as the Giants beat the A's 9 to 4, but it was not that close; it could easily have been 14 or more to 2 or less. The umpiring crew blew easy calls; I say blew because I would not want to accuse them of rooting for the A's. Four clear, easy calls went against us. It was no simple thing to keep our bench at ease after the second one. I saw pitch after pitch, grooved pitches, called balls by the home plate umpire, although Johnny said he was consistent in his calls over the course of the game. I polled our pitchers later on, and they told me that low strikes were called balls so that our pitchers had to elevate the ball upward toward the "happy zone," which is about waist high.

There was never a time I felt anxious about the outcome of the game. The A's, bless their hearts, are the B team, though they did their best to beat us. If only the competition between the teams could be managed so that games between them would be enjoyable.

During the top of the seventh inning a guy I had never talked to before approached me and asked when the soccer players were going to get the field. The soccer players are all Hispanic and are scheduled to get the field at 1pm. It was 1pm, the A's at bat, and I wanted at least for them to finish their part of the inning.

Sitting up against the left field fence, strung out for twenty yards, were the soccer guys. I walked out, got in the center of the line, and pleaded for one half an hour more—1:30pm and we would vacate the field. All along the fence I heard the voices or approval; I thanked them and walked back to the third base dugout and announced the decision.

The A's did not score against Matt White who had relieved Kevin after the fifth inning, the Giants tacked on another run in the bottom of the seventh, and Pete Steele finished off the A's in the top of the eighth. Game over, and we lined up for high fives.

The meeting at the holy mound was quick and upbeat. I asked again that we not rub our win in the face of the A's, and that we would not argue calls and little things that happened in the course of the game. We determined that if A's players complained or criticized certain things that we would listen and not be defensive. I reminded the Giants that any team can beat any other team—such is the game of baseball.

Play the A's again? I don't think so. We will probably slide past this win, but one, two, or three more wins in a row and the peace might be broken. The combination of boredom, anger, hopelessness, meaninglessness, loss of whatever is left of one's youth—these along with the power of athletic competition does not add up to confidence that the peace will hold.[1]

---

1   As it turned out, the two teams played each other one more time with the Giants winning again, and easily. The Giants coaches decided there would be no more games between the teams. The coaches were somewhat divided on the issue, but the players insisted they did not want to play the A's ever again.

9
Sanity vs. Insanity

Mental illness plays large in what happens at San Quentin. I often forget this, however, and it costs me.

Some of the players who were cut from the Giants and then formed the core of the A's I suspect are dealing with emotional troubles. And how could it be otherwise?

Merely being in the misery that is San Quentin has got to impact the psychological well being of any human being. Over the course of four decades, I have seen how exposure to the prison environment affects correctional officers, prison administrators, volunteers, as well as the convicts themselves. Sadly, I have seen seminary students utterly lose their desire or ability to function as a minister. More than a few seminary classmates made shipwreck of their faith after a few years of either working at or serving as a volunteer in the ministry of the Protestant Chapel. I wonder how I am actually doing, and it occurs to me that I have likely not avoided the dangers either.

Some forms of psychosis may develop by being unable to deal with reality, and so a separate reality is constructed that is more easily navigated. The word schizophrenic comes to mind, and it is something I know about, because my youngest brother was so diagnosed in 1968, after he returned from a bad tour in Vietnam.[1]

When I come into the prison for a practice or a game during the week, I head to the Mac Shack, which is positioned right by North Block where most of our players are housed. Those who are physically disabled are sometimes on special diets due to diabetes, for example, and those who are on meds of some sort exit the block first for the chow hall. For years I have watched this group of men shuffle toward the hall and have noticed a number of our ball players in the mix. More than once I have been told by one of our players that so and so is on meds, and therefore be graceful in dealing with them.

---

1   My brother Gary committed suicide about a year after his Army experience. He had been a combat engineer and was on medication at the time.

The convicts who fair the best, in general only I suppose, are those who have had contact with the criminal justice system as juveniles. These often become institutionalized at an early age and fit more easily into adult prisons. But there are many who lived the average middle class life, end up coming to prison, and the adjustment is brutal. Insanity is right around the corner.

On the ball field there is a sense of normalcy to the point that is easy to forget the playing field lies in the heart of a big time prison. The guys seem normal, and many actually are, but the place is ugly and unhealthy despite the department of corrections and rehabilitation's efforts to create a safe environment. It simply cannot be done. Under the surface is pent up anger and rage; sex stuff is always just below the surface, combined with the racial tension—fear, despair, and more is right there all the time.

I do admire and respect those convicts who, after a decade or more in prison, have been able to maintain some sense of sanity and avoid, to some degree, becoming institutionalized. It is better to respect and admire these men than feel sorry for them. It is dangerous to let a convict get into your head to the point you will bring in whatever for them, which happens more often than one would expect.

Insanity can become a place of escape for otherwise normal people, and yes, some do end up in prison. California's laws regarding domestic violence and driving under the influence can result in a couple years in a state pen. And by the way, county time is no piece of cake either and can be worse than state prisons. Once in a while I will find someone who looks like me and talks like me, and I figure it is either a DUI or some kind of domestic violence deal that brought them to prison. These are just the people not prepared for it. From the office to the joint, and it is this group that is most vulnerable for going crazy. Prison can be just that awful.

10

First Loss

May 12, East Bay Lumberjacks Loss 9-0

Nine players, all young studs, with a skinny pitcher who racked up 9 strikeouts, 7 of which were "looking," meaning no swing at the third strike—over seven innings. Three home runs, all long shots sounding like canons being fired. Their defense, offense, and pitching were going, and the catcher had a Buster Posey arm. Real ball players—serious, friendly, baseball guys all the way. Scott Price manages the team—announced he has twin girls on the way.

For the Giants, Mario Ellis started, was fairly sharp but tired quickly. He did not have the arm strength. Johnny's play behind the plate kept us from being embarrassed. Only a couple of errors, but our pitchers—Matt White followed Mario (did not record an out), then Pete came in and was able to stem the flow of runs somewhat. Only two hits for the home team. Guys were frozen with bats in hands at the plate. Duck had a cast on his hand after a surgery to reattach a ligament in his thumb, Bilal pulled a hammy trying to run out a ground ball to short, and Eli with a swollen knee from a slide last game—left us wanting on the bench.

Scott Price's team looks every bit as good as any of the college teams that have come in. And it looked like they were letting up some the last two innings. It's good for our guys to see such a powerful and skilled team, lest they think too highly of themselves.

The team's chemistry is holding solid despite the thumping. If this continues, we will be fine; if not, it could be a long and miserable season.

May 14, Stanislaus Storm, 17-7, Giants have the 7

Another team with nine players, this team up from the Fresno area, meaning they had to be on the road about 4:30am. Louis Quadros runs the team, another power-packed bunch of guys, again as good as any college team I have seen, and the community colleges in the Bay Area field some high quality teams.

Our best pitcher so far, Kevin Driscoll, gave up 10 runs in 3 innings, Frank Braby gave up 2 runs in the next three innings, and Stafont Smith, usually the back-up third baseman, pitched the last 3 innings and gave up 3 runs as well. We had gotten to the desperation point.

Team chemistry—we will see tonight. The thing that complicates it is the A's won one game against The Mission, a team from the City, the evening of May 14, so there will be some discussion about which team ought to really be the A team. Though The Mission, managed by Greg Snyder, cannot be compared to the powerhouse that is the Stanislaus Storm, still the A's will ignore that and merely see a win for them and a loss for us. See, I have developed a we versus they mentality.

I waver between trying to assist the A's and letting them go without scheduling games for them. At this point certain A's players are talking to the outside teams hoping to get games with them and also talking with coaches, both A's and Giants coaches, about getting them games. My feeling is they think I am deliberately sabotaging them, and there may be some truth to it. Elements of the A's are making the season be another unpleasant experience for me, and I am getting tired of it. I can justify my failure to get outside teams to play them by protesting that it is too confusing to schedule games with three other guys doing the same besides working private deals with outside teams that come in.

Tonight we play the East Bay Lumberjacks again, and I will be able to test the chemistry of the team and face A's players who know they have a block of open dates coming up.

11

Two Outs, Nobody On...

...Bottom of the ninth

May 28, Saturday morning, and the A's and the Giants are going at it. At one point I swore that the two teams would not play each other. There is something of a mean streak that runs in me; why can't I just let the guys have fun playing baseball? We have the coaches and the equipment—so what's the matter?

Last Saturday between innings I talked to an A's player and argued that if the A's and Giants played each other ten times and the A's won every single game, that would not make the A's the A team. That designation had to be earned, and it would take a lot longer than one season. The Giants have been playing for eighteen years, and however talented the team might be, or not, the Giants is San Quentin's baseball team.

All along I have been reasonably assured that the Giants are the better team. Testing it by playing a bunch of games and see—that would be meaningless to me but not to about everyone else, probably. Opening day we beat them by eight runs, and it wasn't that close. One umpire made four clearly awful calls resulting in most of the runs the A's scored. The underdog A's have the most fans and unhappily, some of these fans umpire the games. One of my favorite taunts is, "they got ten guys on the field." No one argues differently.

The A's had ten guys on the field again for the second game. Everybody was tense—both sides and the convict fans were close in, watching and listening to every word, studying body language, heckling when possible, trying to get an edge for the A's.

Games at the prison are supposed to be fun for the coaches and the players. But that's hardly the case anymore, far from it. I found myself being tense the whole game. Just underneath the surface the Giants were holding it together. With every bad call from an umpire—balls and strikes, out and safe calls on the bases—soon these could not be counted using fingers alone. The correctional officers must have sensed it as well, as I counted an unusual number of them milling about. One incident and it would be all over. Even one of the officers had confided in me that there was a new Lieutenant in charge, a woman just transferred in from another prison, and she was looking for anything to shut the whole thing down. While lots of cons would be angry at her, she would get the reputation of being tough and would gain esteem from more than half the guards at the prison.

I wished I were somewhere else that day. The score was back and forth. The A's played amazingly well with their key player pitching, whose name I cannot use, because he would not sign a release form for me, and our errors allowed in enough runs to make it scary. For them it meant a chance to get the A team designation, despite everything I had talked to them about earlier. At one point, with the A's ahead by two runs, Junkyard approached me and said that the A's were going to be the A team. I looked at him, I wanted to yell at him and tell him to shut up, but I managed a smile and told him he was being a little premature—the game was not over.

The game went the full nine innings. The soccer guys had to be mollified again, since the game went beyond 1pm, the time when the baseball teams had to vacate the field. Graciously, they understood the importance of the game and yielded. I will say at this point, that generally speaking, the Hispanic prison population is well behaved and congenial. Though I know they all belong to one gang or another, all under the radar or they would be shipped out to another prison better designed custodial wise, I have regularly felt safe with them.

My blood pressure, which is ordinarily normal, was inching upward as I could feel the pressure in my ears. For a moment I had double vision. Not good for me, but there it was, and all I could do was ride it out.

Finally the Giants pulled even in the bottom of the eighth. We got the A's on three quick outs in the top of the ninth, but in the bottom of the inning the Giants made two quick outs. Two outs and nobody on meant we were likely going to have to settle for a tie. The soccer players were getting inpatient.

Johnny, our catcher, a guy whose switch is turned on in the morning and off at night, and in between he is going full blast, walked. First pitch he stole second. Wild pitch he took third. The A's pitcher, Junkyard, was scared to death, and we could all see it. If Johnny scored, the A's would lose, and anything could happen. Eli, a really fast runner, hit a slow dribbler to the short stop, who was playing back too deep. His only chance was to try to get Johnny coming in to home. Good throw, catcher was there blocking the place, lots of dust, but Johnny with his head first slide got the safe call, and that from an umpire who was an A's fan.

I sprinted toward the plate and arrived just as Johnny leaped up with a shout, and it was mayhem joyous. What a win! The celebrating had to be cut short as the soccer guys were taking the field.

The usual high five line-up between the two teams was half-hearted, and I simply went to the dugout and took my cleats off. I was not going to make nice with those guys. A weakness in me I know, but I was not going to do it. I had endured a miserable, tension filled game, and I was not going to ignore my feelings.

We beat the A's two games now. As I gathered the team up on the sacred mound, after the usual recounting of the great plays and contributions to the win, I stated that the two teams would not play again, maybe ever, and that the coaches and I did not want to hear of the teams playing each other without us being there. Well, maybe there would be another game, maybe not, but the coaches would decide the issue.

As we were clearing out of the dugout and getting the gear and uniforms ready to put back into the green metal storage locker, Johnny and Marcus asked to talk with me about playing the A's. They did not share my view of it; they simply wanted to play against a real rival. I understood that, I said, but my concern was that there would be an incident, one that might end the whole sports program. They got it right away, maybe had never seen it from that angle, but they said, "Hey coach, we are with you."

This season held the promise of being a pleasant one. Two games a week for four months with a solid team, interesting guys, talented players, and perhaps the best team I had ever managed at the prison—all jeopardized by the animosity that existed between the teams. Or, was it just me? How much was I contributing to the bad chemistry that existed? Was I really being protective of the program or was it something else, something that resided in me alone?

12
All About Respect

On June 11, the Giants hosted the Santa Monica Suns. This team, perhaps my favorite, has been coming up from Los Angeles for several years. Bob Sharpa is the manager, and most of the players are involved in some way with the film industry. Once I looked out at the mound and saw a face I thought I knew, and it took awhile until I realized I had seen him a number of times in movies.

The Suns arrived on Friday, the day before the game, stayed at local hotels, and were scheduled to play a double header Saturday then head for home on Sunday morning. This year they would play the Giants in the morning and the A's in the evening. I would have preferred two games with the Giants but now we have the B team, the A's, and if I tried to take their Saturday evening field time away from them, there might be a riot.

The way it worked when the Giants played the Suns both games, even if the Suns won in the morning, we usually get them in the evening because I take them to the Marin Brewery in Larkspur for lunch, meaning heavy food and pitchers of beer. They aren't worth much afterwards, so everyone wins.

We all love these guys. They are so much fun to have come in, and the lunch time is the best.

Guillermo, a young Mexican stud pitched for them, eight good innings, then they brought in Jacob, their closer. (Guillermo also hit the game's only home run.) Sharpa played first base well and got a hit. Not bad for an old guy. The team is a mixture of young and middle-aged guys and they work together well. My wife Katie got a photo of the team with me in it, at the East Gate, which I just sent along to Bob.

The game ended in a tie, 8 to 8. We stopped due to the soccer players, who did let us go a half hour longer, since the visiting team had come such a long way. I think the fact that half the Suns were Latinos made a difference, too.

Unbeknownst to the San Quentin ball players, I often email the managers of the teams that come in and get a debriefing. This has proved helpful over the years, as I was able to stop some rather illegal activities from taking place—like the cons asking the visitors to call, write, email, or otherwise contact various friends and family members. Then I have found that visiting players have given inmates batting gloves, baseball gloves, cleats, and even clothing items. A lot of times I will catch this when it is happening and ask Stan Damas, the enforcer, to take care of the problem.

Stan, ex San Francisco cop, ex head of security for Bill Graham presents, mid-seventies now, handles all problems. He roams the lower yard doing business. My old friend, he makes all the difference.

Bob and I talked Sunday, the day after the game. What he told me I should have been prepared for, but I wasn't. Well, I had suspected, but I really thought the A's players would be above such things. They are not. They are the B team, and they proved it again. Although Bob did not know their names, I was watching what was going on behind the visiting dugout during the game. The Suns got a complete running account from some A's players of which Giants liked what pitches and how to defend the various hitters. Bob did not say if they were giving the Suns Giant's signs, but my guess is they did try. The Suns would have none of it. They were offended and disappointed. They agreed that these guys were the B team. No respect was the consensus.

Respect is a big deal in prison like anywhere else, but in prison it looms larger. To give respect is to honor and value. Where there is no respect, a dangerous environment is created, and anything can happen.

The A's did not respect themselves. They did not act honorably. The A's did not respect the Suns; the Suns would not take advantage of the Giants by listening to the A's information. The A's did not respect the game, either. The A's once again proved they were the B team.

Hoping the Suns would beat the Giants, the A's players thought this would elevate them as a team. I would like to sit down with the A's players and talk to them about this, but an argument would likely break out. At least I will gather the Giants together tomorrow night and talk to them about it. I am hoping that no Giants players did the same during the game that evening. Bob did not say there was a problem, and I would be surprised if any Giant attempted to pass along information about the A's.

To respect the game of baseball means respecting those who play the game, watch the game, love the game. It is not small thing.

One other thing Bob told me—the A's beat the Suns, 6 to 5. He said that once the A's got ahead they stopped the game, although there was plenty enough time for another inning. He said, "Oh well." And I said, "Yes, the B team."

13

Johnny and Curtis

"I played with the Astros in the seventies," an old con told me, "And I can still throw the ball a hundred miles an hour."

"Number 8, that was my number when I was in the big leagues."

"I was a Yankee, played with Don Mattingly in the glory years."

My response is often "Okay, let me check that on the internet. How do you spell your name?"

Maybe I would create a fictional life if I were spending most of the years of my life in prison. I think everyone wants to be somebody and have purpose and meaning in life, even if it is a fantasy. Usually, I just listen and act impressed.

There are only a few players on the Giants that I trust enough to tell their stories in a book like this. I am told so many lies, which is understandable, since so many felons do not want to appear in a bad light. But with Johnny and Curtis, I will take the risk.

Johnny is thirty-eight years old, has been in prison for eighteen years, and is not eligible for parole until 2029. He is white, but ran with the Hispanics and is classed with that race. He looks every bit the convict—tattoos on his neck, arms, chest, and back. To me he looks like he has fetal alcohol syndrome, meaning his mother drank to excess while Johnny was in the womb.

He is bright, however, and very active, an excellent athlete, and very much a dedicated Giants player. He is one of those guys who gives it all he's got. Physically he is a wreck. His knees both need replacing, and I understand at least one will be done after the season is over. Around the seventh inning on a hot day, maybe two more innings to go, and Johnny won't come out of the game. He has learned to ignore the pain, which I can see in his face and movements once in a while.

However, Johnny is easily angered. He tries to keep it under control, but it flashes out now and then. He and Mario will get into some real scary arguments, and I have to get in the middle of it for fear that the lower yard officers will make a report about it. He told me, and I guess it is common knowledge, that he killed more than one person, maybe a few, and he knows he earned the years he has to do.

Last week he saw his son, Little John, for the first time in six years. The son, now eighteen, has grown up without a father, and the mother, Johnny's wife, is divorcing him. Not unusual when a wife has waited nearly two decades already and is facing a couple more of these. Johnny wears jersey #29, and he asked me if I could find another Giants jersey with #29 on it and send it to his son. Along with eight photos of Johnny taken on Opening Day, the jersey was sent off priority mail yesterday.

Curtis, aged forty-nine, is a three striker, and a parole hearing scheduled for 2029 would seem like a big break for him. He is not eligible for parole until 2044. Three strikes, three felony convictions, earns a long stretch in prison. The law is peculiar to California and was an effort by the voters to put the worst criminals away for a long time. It probably works, but it also condemns many non-violent offenders, who may be capable of being rehabilitated, to a situation that is hopeless.

At the beginning of the baseball season I handed out a sheet of paper to the Giants players on which I had some questions about their lives. Curtis' response was by far the most extensive. At age six he was molested by an older brother, which continued for many years, and which was followed by his father sexually abusing him as well. Very sordid, so much so I wish I had never read it. Though he married and fathered two children, his life was a mess.

Curtis liked to smoke crack cocaine; it destroyed his life. He robbed places, small time stuff, to get money for drugs. Once he burglarized a relative's cabin in Big Bear, southern California resort area, and picked up a strike. Strike one, a robbery in 1985, strike two, another robbery in 1989 (Curtis claims he did not do it), and this last one got him a nine year sentence, but he did only five due to good behavior. Strike three was a robbery, and a fourth strike a burglary—both in 1995. His sentence was fifty years to life. What he needed was rehabilitation in an appropriate setting.

His wife divorced him, he has lost contact with his parents, and he doubts he will ever go home—he has no home to go to anyway. He is convinced he will die in prison and hopes it will be sooner rather than later. From time to time he is placed on suicide watch.

He never feels safe from the sexual predators. He is a small man, and now nearly fifty he is an easy target. He has been raped in prison more than once and lives in constant fear of being attacked. To this day, he is constantly worried about it happening again and cannot get it off his mind. Unfortunately, he has no group he runs with and is forced into being somewhat of a loner.

Curtis is a Christian but does attend chapel services. The last chaplain treated him so poorly that he is soured on the whole chapel experience.

A few games back, Curtis brought me a letter from a prison doctor—no more throwing baseballs for him. He had surgery to reattach a ligament in his right shoulder, but when I asked that he play second base he said yes and did, despite the pain. Curtis will now take over the 3rd base coaching box and give the signs which I will flash from the safety of the dugout. Hope I am not putting Curtis in harm's way, but I cannot see the ball coming off those aluminum bats anymore, plus it gives him an active role on the team.

There is a three striker who plays on the A's, and I am glad he received a long sentence. We are all a little safer with him behind bars. Curtis, on the other hand, in my view anyway, should have been released a long time ago. The difference between the two men illustrates the near impossibility of creating a level playing field in terms of corrections and rehabilitation. On paper, both convicts look the same, but they are radically different from one another, and the prison system, despite its growing sophistication, is not equipped to deal with the nuances.

14

It Was a Tsunami

Thursday, June 16 will be a hard day to forget or remember.

A new team was coming in called Tsunami, managed by Daniel Larson. Looking over the ages of the players, I knew it was going to be a tough game, since the guys were young. Most of them lived in San Francisco's Mission District, in the area that was enjoying a resurgence, and where a lot of young techy types were moving.

As I drove down into the prison's visitor's parking lot I spotted them right away, especially one tall, well built young man. Turned out he left his photo ID at home and would not get in. He said he would walk over to the Larkspur ferry terminal and catch a boat back to the City. Picturing the long and potentially dangerous walk, I told him I would drive him over there, since there was still plenty of time left before I had to escort the Tsunami into the prison.

On the way, Stuart is his name, said he was going to be the starting pitcher and Daniel would have to go with someone else. Right away I felt a slight bit of disappointment, as I would rather face a team's best. Most baseball people would rather lose to a team's best than beat something less. Stuart assured me that the other guy would be tough on us in any case.

Tsunami's left hander, John Hirsch, was that all right, but he could not find the strike zone quickly enough and we scored two runs in the first inning, which would prove to be enough for a Giants' win. During the second inning, however, one of the worst mishaps took place I have ever seen at the prison.

Kevin Loughlin was running the game and was at the 3rd base coaching box making the calls; I was at the first base box. Bottom of the second, a runner on first base, no one out, and Kevin flashes the steal sign. Our runner, Stafont Smith, takes off, the Tsunami catcher fired down to second but the ball skipped off just behind the second baseman. He turned to retrieve the ball, took a few steps, and collapsed. Looked like an ankle to me, and I ran toward him. He was face down moaning in agony. I knelt beside him and looked him over. I had been a medic in the military for four years and still remembered some of what I had been taught.

Not wanting to touch him, I asked him where it hurt. No answer but he gestured with his hand toward his feet. It was quite easy to see there was a bulging on the sock just above his cleat on his right foot. Not a compound fracture as there was no blood or broken skin; it was as though the bone had snapped in a clean, straight line, surgically straight.

The player, Jay Hardaway, the only black on the Tsunami, thirty years old, slight of build, strong and wiry, wore long and carefully braided dreads, with plenty of tattoos on his arms. (Later on, waiting for the ambulance, Jay explained the tattoos, which turned out to be mostly names of his family grouped about with a big cross.)

Right away an officer ran toward us and I asked him to call for an ambulance. I was not sure if Jay knew what had happened to him. I was checking for signs of shock, none of which had appeared, and I just kept him talking to me.

Soon a whole crowd gathered about us on the grass, about fifteen yards from the second base bag. An Alarm sounded, meaning that the inmates had to sit down. Almost all of the Giants were seated in the dugout since we had been at bat with the exception of Stafont Smith who had stolen second and was sitting on the bag watching the events unfold. Stafont usually had a big toothy grin going, but now he was somber looking.

San Quentin's own ambulance arrived. A couple of the guys I knew were part of the crew. The free man, the supervisor of the paramedic team, looked at Jay's injury and made a call to an outside ambulance that could transport Jay to Marin General Hospital in Greenbrae because he knew surgery would be required.

A good twenty minutes went by before the ambulance arrived. It had to go through the vehicle sally port for inspection first. The two paramedics from St. Joseph's Ambulance service surveyed the situation quickly, carefully took the cleat on Jay's right foot off, cut away the sock, and stabilized the ankle and foot. Then they used an "air" splint, a clear plastic pillow-like contraption. Jay did not react much to it but clung to a baseball I had given him.

Just before the St. Joseph's ambulance arrived, Kevin brought a baseball out that all the Giants players had signed. Jay saw it, kissed it, and lifted up his arm and waved the ball at the Giants' dugout. All the guys applauded like crazy. I wish I could more appropriately express this.

After some few minutes, Jay was lifted onto a gurney and loaded into the back of the ambulance. Once more the Giants' applause could be heard. One of the other Tsunami players climbed into the ambulance and went along with Jay. Play resumed after some warm ups and a few innings later, the Giants recorded the win.

But the real tsunami had struck earlier.

Kevin Driscoll figured he would never get out of prison. Sentenced to fifty years[1] he would respond to the question, "When are you going home?" with, "Never!" It had been murder by gun, and Kevin was in his mid-thirties. Even if he one day walked out or was wheeled out, what kind of a life would he have? No home, no family, nothing really; maybe it would be better to die in prison.

On Saturday, June 11, five days before the Tsunami game, I brought my wife Katie into the prison with me. She had been there a number of times before, the most recent being opening day, May 7. She had met Kevin then along with the rest of the team. When we got home Saturday afternoon she commented on how strange Kevin had been. I said I saw the wild look in his eye, too. He started on the mound, had two good innings, and then fell apart in the third. Needing to keep his bat in the game, I put him at second base, but he did not field or hit well. That's the background then for what would follow on Tuesday, the 14th.

---

[1] Kevin, upon his return home from a business trip, got in a fight with his wife; she was angry and fought hard. Kevin reached into his night stand, pulled out his home security weapon and shot her. He got 25 years for the murder and a 25 year enhancement for using a gun. Had he used a baseball bat he would have been looking at a 25 to life sentence instead. I verified all this with his father at a lunch at Marin Brewery early in the year. Kevin had just completed the work for a law degree. I doubt he will ever get to take a bar exam.

15

The Con?

Paul Newman and Robert Redford starred in "The Sting," a con run by experts. "Con" comes from convict, and cons run cons as a kind of sport. Prison is boring, among other things, and anything that concentrates the mind and provides some excitement is welcomed. Over the years I have been conned, never saw it coming, only realized it after the fact, and I thought I was experienced enough now to keep out of harm's way. I was almost wrong.

In the days following Kevin's beating I heard more reports of what had happened. Some discrepancies became apparent, however. For instance, the number of officers beating on him declined sharply. Reasons for the incident were talked about, and I began to think that Kevin had even provoked the officers involved, to some degree. Other details did not match up, and my mind went to the possibility of a con being run on me.

I have to admit that some of the convicts would like to get rid of me. It has been attempted in the past, and the trouble I am having with some A's players might be a motive for another try at it. They think, and I know this for certain, that I am favoring the Giants. Truth is, I am. It all has to do with scheduling games. That job was taken away from me for the first time in fifteen years, and I resent it. More than that, it complicates my world, so I let the chips fall where they may, which has meant that in the past two months the A's have played far fewer games than the Giants. I could have prevented it, but I didn't.

Prison, for both prisoner and guard, likely will corrupt the mind, however subtlety, but bending or distorting it is certain. Though this is a subject I often mention or allude to, I continue to bring it up, because I know I have been impacted but I do not know to what degree. Am I being paranoid thinking a con is being run on me? I talk to my wife about it, and she is not sure either. As I write this, I can sense some anger in me. I can't let that stupid prison make me crazy.

Back to Kevin: the most graphic and horrific accounts came from two A's players. Both insisted on talking to me where the officer in the gun tower just above the field might be able to hear, and if not that, certainly he would be able to observe the description of the beating being acted out for my benefit. It is also well known that I have a tendency to over-react, even go off sometimes, and it dawned on me that if I were provoked to take the inmate's side and start accusing the prison officials with gross injustice and law breaking—prisoners do have rights and court ordered protections—I might just get bounced out of the prison. A game within a game?

A con? Right now I am not sure, but I am suspicious. I am going to slow it down, focus on listening and keeping my mouth shut. However, one thing I will do: I am going to work on moving the A's back to the intramural status as originally intended. I've got my plan; I have to have a survival plan. If I am going off the deep end, then I have to move back from the edge. It is far more difficult for me to give it up all together than make a change I calculate will lessen my anxiety. Maybe I am too invested.

There is something else, too. All it would take to have my beige (brown) card pulled and my tenure as the baseball coach ended would be for a con to accuse me of groping him or something similar. I would quickly be gone and could even face criminal charges. If I were to land in some lock-up, I would not last long.

16
Softball Swing

Prisoners play a lot of softball; few play baseball. The softball played is slow pitch, where the ball is arched 6 to 9 feet in the air, and the batter will use an exaggerated upper cut to hit the steeply falling ball. Often the batter will "step in the hole" meaning that the back foot is moved backward and downward suddenly during the swing. The result of it is that the head moves a great deal. This does not matter much in slow pitch softball, but it is death in fast pitch hardball.

The issue is that the head moves way too much for a batter with a softball swing to hit a baseball thrown at seventy miles per hour or faster. The brain tracks the trajectory of the ball, and with reasonable hand-eye coordination, the bat will meet the ball. Or, at least a good baseball swing with less head movement has a better chance to put a ball in play.

Adrian "Red" Casey, a Black man with red hair and blue eyes, our captain, number four hitter and first baseman, due to playing softball for many years, understandably stepped up with an awful softball-style swing. For a couple of years he was going for the home run record, which is 13, but in the last twelve games this year he is batting under 200 with no homers. Red and I have had our disagreements over the years. Indeed, for two seasons he was mad at me and only talked to me if he had to. Last week I could see he was desperate.

Red was voted the team captain this year over last year's choice, Johnny Taylor, for the first time ever. Two games in a row I took him out of the game for a player whom I hoped might have a better chance of putting the ball in play. Red no longer had that coveted clean-up role. Before I made the moves, I told Red what was happening, and he just looked at me and nodded. He knew why.

A week ago, June 20, I asked Red if I could talk to him about his swing. Not that I know that much about hitting a baseball, but I ended up playing in two scrimmage games and was hitting .500 with only one strike out. Not bad for a sixty-nine year old guy. Funny thing, the players paid more attention to my instruction after that, and Red did too. He wanted some help.

I showed him what I knew. Negative load, front foot down first before the swing begins, arms in close, swing almost straight down, level the bat through the zone, then a slight up with the bat in the follow through. That and discipline yourself as best you can about what to swing at—unless, of course, you have two strikes on you already—and swing at pitches you can hit without reaching hard it. Standard stuff, taught at most high schools, standard in college and professional levels, but not the rule in prisons due to the softball swing.

The lesson lasted less than two minutes. Red grabbed the bat out of my hands and said, "I got it coach; I'll have it for next game."

He did, too—well not the next game but this very last one. It took him a little longer to adjust than he thought. I could not have done it. I barely have it down, and I was at it seemingly forever before I was able to keep myself from striding while swinging. For fifty-plus years I have been swinging the bat wrong, so that if I hit it, it would largely be an accident. It took a "re-patterning" of my muscles and my mind.

I'm proud of Red, surprised too. Murder 2—long, long sentence, not sure he will ever get out, but as a muscular solid athlete hitting from the left side it sure will be nice to see him loft a few over our short-porch in right field.

17
Full Blast Rivalry

What started it all? How did it get to this point?

I can only guess at what happened, but I think it goes back to 2004 when all the media attention began.[1]

There were rumors that I was in danger. I would need to step back, as I heard it. I did not, since I did not see or feel any real problem.

Prior to the start of the 2005 season a big meeting was planned. Word was that I was bumped from managing the Giants, and the powers that be intended to reshape the program. To counter, I suggested the formation of a second team, a resurrection of the old Pirates, which I would manage, thus leaving an un-named person to manage the Giants.

Coming into the prison for the big meeting, I was stunned to find that my brown card was not in its normal place at the East Gate. The officer at the gate, a person I had known for many years, explained that an un-named person had pulled it out of the box only moments before. I asked to make a call from the phone in the east gate shack and try to contact the person who was putting the meeting together. That move got me into the prison, into the meeting, and manager of the Pirates.[2]

It was not long before I found out the reason for the trouble: media attention, and all the cons knew it. It was intolerable to the un-named person that I should be getting the attention, although there wasn't really much of it. However, unbeknownst to me, a documentary was planned for filming the baseball team, and though I had managed the team alone for years, a change had to be made.

Put a camera in front of someone's face and magic happens. Nearly

---

1   I wish I could be more concrete, but I cannot. People and places could certainly be named and things said, yet it is necessary to be vague. We are talking about prisons and convicts, and convicts often get paroled.

2   The original San Quentin team was the Pirates. The Pirates became the Giants when the San Francisco Giants gave us their winter uniforms.

everyone succumbs. I am not immune either. During the late 1960s and early 1970s I had my share. A leader in the Jesus People Movement, I had made Time magazine and even had some television interviews. For years I had travelled with a band called Joyful Noise and flew around the country like a big deal. After awhile it all passed and I never realized anything out of it except grief and disillusionment. Sure, I was a little resentful at being brushed aside, but that feeling did not last too long. Most ball players wish the press would just go away, unless you are a convict playing outside teams in a famous prison.

That was then, after which things returned to normal for several years. Having one team, the Giants, much of the media attention went away, and things were good. Then it started up all over again, and the rush to mug in front of a lens changed things—at least, this is part of the equation as it seems to me.

Red Sox versus the Yankees, Dodgers versus the Giants—historic rivalries, and we love them. San Quentin Giants versus the San Quentin A's—some love it, and I would like to love it, but there is no real history to it, no naturalness to it, no fun to it either. But it rages and it is getting to me. I can see myself deteriorating, see myself losing my balance. Stress is a killer, and I am stressed out to the point of becoming combative. Something has to be done.

18

Convict Mentality

The good, the bad, and the ugly. A cliché I know, but it fits.

Some of the finest people I have ever known are convicts. I think of Chris Rich, who killed his wife with a baseball bat. He fell into alcohol dependence after his very promising baseball career ended. If you spent some time with him, you would know why I think so highly of him, and it all started out on a bad note, because I identified him as part of the reason I got bounced for a couple seasons from the Giants to the A's. He even confessed his part in it to me.

Bilal Chatman, a Muslim[1] and a man I trust who has consistently been a credit to the Giants. When he lost his starting position due to lack of production at the plate, his positive presence on the bench was noticeable. And what a face! His character shines through. I nicknamed Bilal "The Rock." I wish I had spent a lot more time than I did just talking with him, and now I may never have the chance.

Chris Marshall, Marcus Crumb, Stafont Smith, Doug Winn, Orlando "Duck" Harris, Mike Tyler, Charles Lyons, all Black like Bilal and YaYa—I include these men among the "good." A Black A's player, Marvin Andrews is also a fine man I have known for years—they don't come any better. And there are others I could mention but who did not have a chance to sign a release form.

A Pacific Islander, another designated racial group at the prison, is Eli Sala. A quiet man, stocky, strong, not fat, a gold tooth right in front. He can hit, run, and field. He can also pitch. For years now he has been on one of my teams, and even though he can only show up on Saturdays due to classes he takes during the week, I welcome him on the team anyway. From time to time I hear complaints from other Giants about Eli's unavailability for Thursday night games.

---

1   Interesting that I am a Christian, and two of my staunchest supporters have been Muslims during this tumultuous 2011 season—Bilal and YaYa. Both African Americans, converts to Islam, and have consistently proven themselves to be reliable and honorable men.

Eli is like gold, like the tooth. He is not the best guy ever to be in a SQ Giants uniform, but he will always be an MVP to me.

Curtis Roberts and Pete Steele are men I have gotten to know well. Also there is Frankie Smith, our first base coach—a fine man, who I just heard has been diagnosed with head and neck cancer, which has spread throughout his jaw and lower mouth. Stage four, I think someone said; it seems improbable now that I will ever see him again.

In one of the last games I managed before being forced out, Frankie pitched for the opposing team. Only seven players showed up and without a pitcher or catcher. Marcus volunteered to catch and Frankie to pitch. He must be fifty-five and had likely not been throwing; nevertheless, he pitched five solid innings and only gave up three runs, which was enough for a loss, but what heart he displayed! By the fourth inning I could see he was in pain; he sucked it up and keep firing.

Pete Steele deserves a whole chapter devoted just to him. He is the con who came out of nowhere to pitch for what were the Pirates ten years ago and win that game throwing to Donnie Worthy behind the plate. Later that year we lost Pete when it was discovered he had created a document, somehow, forged a captain's signature, and was able to get himself from H Unit up to the lower yard after the restrictions placed on him for some kind of mischief. Then, after the season, he disappeared, only to show up again in May of this year and has become our most dependable pitcher.

Pete can play anywhere: pitcher, first base, short stop, third base, outfield, and he is so far the home run champ. Tall and strong, now forty years old, athletic but does not necessarily look it, he took a bad hop during a game, was hit right in the mouth, blood everywhere and a front toot punctured his lower lip. Hideous injury and away he went in an ambulance. That was on a Thursday, but that next Saturday, he pitched nine whole innings and won the game for the Giants, even hit a homer.

Meth has been Pete's and many other con's problem; that drug is so hard to resist. I have been told that it would take hold of me, too, if I ever tried it. The whites like meth—it speeds them up for working, sex, and fighting. Matt White, Frank Braby, and Pete—each decent men, not bad or ugly, but the attraction is powerful. Pete has a wife, kids, a home, and a job waiting for him. It sounds like he has started going to the chapel, and he really wants to make it. He's a likeable guy and will be going home here in the same county where I live at the end of August, and I hope he gives me a call.

I did not mention Mario Ellis and have not said much about Mike or

Charles, but they are also fine men. Mario, a superior athlete, is hard to manage. He redefines "defensive." Mike and Charles are not great baseball players but will be stars on the football team. They are, without a doubt, the fastest guys in the prison.

I can't go too far discussing the "bad" ones, and I don't want to judge. Who knows what any man would do given the conditions they have to live with. Take away hope and meaning, and what is left? Prison is a place where struggles are being fought even to maintain one's humanness. Not to have any real goal, or mission as it is often put, robs a man of something that goes to the core. It is possible that a mission might be to try to cause the collapse of the baseball program. All the guys who have been cut from making a team over the years or those who have proven to others and even themselves that they just don't have it anymore—the search for meaning goes on.

I have heard a lot of sad stories, usually second-hand, since convicts rarely carry on much. Stoic might describe it. There is danger in over-sympathizing with the convicts. It's not uncommon to see hear of someone naively trying to make a convict's life a little better by bringing in some form of contraband. Innocent, ignorant, and foolish, which then becomes criminal and illegal. I will never forget the seventy-two year old woman who, as a long time volunteer with the Protestant Chapel, brought in items that actually led to her arrest. I knew this fine woman well, and I will not easily get out of my mind the sight of her being taken out of the building that houses the warden and the other higher-ups in hand cuffs, being escorted to a waiting police car. Strangely, I never heard of her again—nothing but silence.

The ugly—there is ugliness in everyone, me included. Ugly lies hidden in wait, because it is costly to display it. I see it more plainly in some of the correctional officers. Among these are the good; I would like to talk about them but I should not. Every convict knows the good cops, and these men and women are respected. The good ones are firm, fair, and approachable. They do their jobs, obey the rules, and are not mean. The bad and the ugly are perhaps the majority. The worst are those who have to show they are tough by being mean and vengeful. They play the ubiquitous game of payback. They have not internalized the golden rule of treating others as you would be treated.

Due to my longevity at San Quentin, I have seen officers turned and changed. At the start they are pleasant, business-like, but human. Over time, I have seen the move from good to bad. And it is ugly.

19

Our Captains Have Fallen

Red quit the team the first week in August, the second to last game I was with the team before my exit.

Not the easiest man to get along with, Red was one of the few convicts I could be a little afraid of. Powerfully built, he could get a strange look in his eye. More than once he had utterly stopped communicating with me. For two years he would verbally accost me during games while I was coaching the flag football team and start in on some harangue, the meaning of which I could never grasp, though I tried to make sense of the nature of the trouble.

Red was elected captain by the team for 2011. Johnny had been the captain in 2010, but for reasons unknown, he was rejected. When I heard about it, I was not pleased. Johnny was the guy I would confide in, and he could be depended on to tell me the truth. Now he had been replaced.

Being captain means little more than handling internal complaints among the players, so the coaches are not burdened with them. I don't think Red saw the job that way; what he wanted to do was to hassle the players for making errors in the field and not hitting at the plate.

This misunderstanding of his role surfaced in June. The Giants lost a couple of games back-to-back, which always spells trouble, and Red was harassing players in the dugout for their errors. Seeing this, I took Red aside and explained that, at least during a game, we do not get on players for either physical or mental mistakes—it is a coaching thing to be worked out in a practice. Red strongly disagreed, and the conversation ended dismally. However, Red did stop the confrontations with the players, but only for a while.

I'm not sure how old Red is, early forties at least, but his skills are declining. For years he had the number four hole in the line-up. Clean-up is how we like to designate it, and there is pressure to perform. Red's performance began to slip until it disappeared. This was when I worked with him on his hitting, and it improved to some degree. That lasted only a few games ,then he fell back into the old way of swinging, the softball swing, and it was painful for everyone to watch. There was no choice. Kevin, our great co-manager and long-time friend, and I agreed—Red had to be moved to a lower hole in the batting order. I can see the look on his face right now when he came into the dugout to look at the line-up card, as though he knew what he would find. Yep, batting seventh. He never said a word and proceeded to go hitless in three at-bats with one strike out.

The next game it started again; he was getting into player's faces if they made an error. It sounded mean and degrading, so I had to ask him to step outside the dugout for a little chat. This was not an exciting time for me. He would not listen but insisted as captain he had the right to rebuke and reprove team players. He walked away from me in mid stream.

The next game we played a tough team and were behind from the first inning. Red was at first base, hitting sixth now because Kevin and I wanted to give him something, and he was playing badly, two errors in the field, two strike-outs looking, but worse, dogging it, and Kevin would have none of it.

This was a game I was running, and I was at the third base coaching box. After an inning's third out, the team broke from the dugout toward their defensive positions, all except Red. He sauntered late out to first, with no baseball in his glove for warming the infielders up, and Kevin yelled out to him to hustle it up. Soon as he heard it, Red stopped, turned, threw his glove toward the dugout, tore off his cap, jerked off his shirt right about when he got alongside the pitcher's mound, and that was it. He quit.

Kevin approached him and the two got in a terrific argument, which drew the attention of a lower yard officer. If a fist fight were to break out, or even some shoving, the whole program might suffer. I entered the dugout and tried to quiet the men, and failing that, I told them that a cop was approaching. That at least cooled things down, but Red was gone.

What a shock, but it was not over. The trouble spilled over to the rest of the guys, and a heated argument erupted between Johnny and Kevin. By that time, I was out at third base again and did not know what was taking place. At the end of the inning there was no Johnny in the dugout—he had quit the team, too.

I was crushed; I felt empty. My confidant on the team was gone. The captain was gone. We got beat and badly. Team chemistry was gone, and where do we go from here?

20

Bullies

Prey or predators, it will be one or the other.

If you are weak you can be taken advantage of. Maybe it will be desserts handed over, money for the cantine, maybe clothes, maybe sex.

Brutal, mean, and cruel are words that describe the animal kingdom. It also describes prison life. Without a "car," meaning a group of people that you belong to, a convict is vulnerable.

Gangs are a way of life, even if you are in a prison where known gang members are shipped out to prisons better able to provide higher levels of custody. It is mostly racial—blacks, whites, Hispanics, Pacific Islanders, and a few other smaller tribes. Sociologists study tribal behavior, and they would only have to spend some time in a prison to find a good sample to run a study on.

Old cons will have demands made on them by younger, tougher cons. The old guys, without backing, can be made into sexual slaves. Strong language? I don't think so. The weak, the gang-less, the tribe-less—these become prey.

Race, sex, drugs, and power are the driving forces of prison life. Race is the larger tribe; being a member of a dominate race brings power, power to get what you want, mostly sex and drugs, but also smaller favors.

Every convict who comes into the prison is scouted by other cons to determine their power position. Even the buff, strong looking guys are vulnerable without a gang identity. Sometimes cons will claim an incoming inmate as a sex punk before they even arrive. This is not lost on the administration, and there are segregation cells for those who ask for protection due to one thing or another, but the predators most often, eventually have their way.

This chapter is titled "bullies," which is not a prison term but a contemporary word used in the society at large. Bullies are active in schools, from elementary all the way to college, but mostly among the younger kids. Finding a weakness in another is a kid's game. I remember telling bullies even at Woodlawn Grammar School in Portland, Oregon, during the 1940s, "My dad can beat up your dad." In high school I was bullied all the way until my senior year. I know what it is like, and I hate it. When I became a man, I refused to give in to anyone; I will stand up for myself even if it means getting the crap beat out of me. This attitude has gotten me into a lot of trouble at San Quentin.

Perhaps my intolerance to going along to get along is why I have survived thirty years as a volunteer at the prison. Maybe, but it sure has landed me solidly in the trouble I am in now. I refuse to give into the bullies who made demands on me, accuse me of racism, and put out death threats against me. Throw me out completely, okay, but I am not going to bend over so I can keep my beige volunteer card.

Someone might ask, "How could a convict bully a volunteer?" Let me count the ways. One, plant a contraband item in a coach's equipment bag. Two, accuse the coach of over-familiarity like groping or something akin to that. Three, accuse the coach of bringing items in to favored inmates, again, over-familiarity but more serious. Four, have friends on the outside make unwelcome contact with the volunteer. Five, start a rumor campaign designed to defame a coach, which it appears is happening to me right now.

This last one may seem less serious than the others, but to me it is not. My reputation is important to me, and I will stand up for it. The trouble is that, at the prison, volunteers have little opportunity to address the issues brought up in rumors. The prison officials don't have the time or the obligation to investigate for the truth. Often the accusation of a convict will be enough. No appeal, no chance to confront an accuser, no defense at all. The inmates are aware of this and use it to their advantage. Bully all they want, and it rarely results in any discipline.

Most volunteers come into a prison like San Quentin to do some good and are naïve about the dynamics swirling about them. So many quit when they feel the pressure; others are not able to and become foils, the ducks cons love to __uck.

Again, the reality is that there are the good, there are the ugly, and there are the bad.

21

One in the Face

Baseball can be a dangerous game. Some have even died.

A baseball is hard and only 9 inches in circumference. A pitcher can throw a pitch 100 miles an hour, though this is rare. Major leaguers are often clocked in the mid-to-high nineties, and a change-up will dip into the low eighties. A pitch thrown at ninety mph can be batted back to the pitcher faster than it was thrown.

A bat is made of wood, hard wood, and is an incredible weapon, if so desired. The prison no longer allows bats to be on the grounds; our coaches have to bring them in for every game and practice and leave with them.

More injuries occur when a ball is hit or in trying to catch them. Baseball requires a complicated set of skills—running, throwing, sliding, and hitting are only the tip of the iceberg. These may come in combinations and quickly force the body's joints, ligaments, tendons, and muscles to extreme stress. Our 17-man Giants team has anywhere from one to five players with some kind of injury.

One law of baseball is that when you are on the field or near it, keep your eye on the ball. Stan failed to keep the rule.

Every other Monday evening the Giants get the field for a practice; the A's get the alternate Monday and so on. Due to injuries there were two guys working out at new positions. Mike Tyler was at first, a position he had never played before, and Duck Harris was at second, just coming back from surgery to his left thumb. They needed practice, and I was hitting them ground balls with Frankie Smith catching for me.

The baseball diamond is situated so that the sun goes down behind right field, a little to the right of Mt. Tamalpais, which can be seen from the field. Stan wanted to talk to Frankie, no doubt dealing with some issue, and he simply walked up to him while Mike made a throw in from first base. Mike's throw was high and off target. Bang! It hit Stan near his right eye, just a smidgen above it, and down Stan went.

Stan is seventy-five at least—strong, wiry, and in good shape—but down he went. The ball was not thrown terribly hard, but there was Stan lying in the dust almost on home plate, and there was blood. I flung my bat in the dirt, not sure why I did that, must have been frustration, and I knelt beside Stan. I looked to find Mike and could not. Turned out he went immediately to the dugout and sat down.

When blood is spilled, it is a big deal at the prison. An officer, who knew Stan well, rushed over and called for a medic. I made a quick exam and thought it was no big deal, but who knew. Protocol took over, and Stan would have to go to the hospital, not the prison hospital, but Marin General in Greenbrae and for reasons I am not sure of.

Stan complied, as he was a little shaken up by the blow to the head, and he said he would call his wife Alberta to meet him at the hospital. Off he went then and the practice proceeded.

Mike was very fleet of foot but a terrible base runner and did not start or play in many games. He would mope around, and at times I thought he might quit the team, but he held on. His sport is football, and he had played on the flag football team I started some years earlier called The Blues Brothers and would play for my son Vern who was now running that team. But baseball—Mike mostly sat on the bench.

One look at him, and it was plain he was thunder struck by what happened. Mike was one of Stan's favorites and vice versa. Mike felt so bad, all he would do was sit and look glum.

Practice ends right about 7:30, and Stan had been transported to the hospital at about 6. Just as we were packing up, all of a sudden there was a commotion at the entrance to the dugout. It was Stan, back with a bandage over his eye and forehead, but there he was, and he was hugging Mike. And there were tears in Mike's eyes but a big smile on his face. Stan and Mike were actually jumping up and down together. Quite a scene.

I caught part of the conversation between the two. Mike was apologizing, and Stan was telling him it was okay, assuring Mike that it was a pure accident and that he never should have been on the field talking to Frankie in the first place.

Stan, the retired cop, had arrested plenty of black kids like Mike during his career. Mike had no doubt hated and feared white cops growing up as a gang banger in the Bay Area. The old white cop and the young black banger. Stan told me later as we were going up cardiac hill that he would never forget the tears in Mike's eyes.

22
Curtis and the Justice

Curtis is one of the cons I will miss most. Often on suicide watch, takes meds, had one testicle recently removed due to a cancerous growth, has nobody on the outside anymore, knows he will die in prison, is constantly having to avoid sexual predators, and is forced into being a loner now that he has made a decision to separate himself from the Protestant Chapel, for what I think are good reasons.

A couple months ago, I brought my wife Katie in for a Saturday morning ball game. She is a big baseball fan, and we enjoy following the San Francisco Giants. We talk often of Huffy Puffy (Aubrey Huff), Buster Posey and how we miss him due to the injury, along with Freddie Sanchez, Pat Burrell, Andres Torres, Timmy, Matt, Vogelsong, Madison, the Panda, Aaron, Cody, Nate the Great, all the guys, and we worry about Barry and Jonathan and Eli. Brian Wilson, Jeremy Affeldt, Sergio Romo—the torture guys—we love them. And we love the new nickname for Brandon Belt, Baby Giraffe, and on it goes. We would elect Bruce Bochy president and be sure to have cabinet posts for Ron Wotus, Tim Flannery, Roberto Kelly, Dave Righetti, Mark Gardner, and of course, Mike Murphy, without whom we would not have a Giants baseball team. Of course, we hang on every word from Kruk, Kuip, John, and Dave—people we think are just as important to the team as the coaches and players. Okay, enough of that.

Katie wanted to keep score but knew she needed help. I brought Curtis over, sat him down beside her—they have known each other for years—and they spent the entire rest of the game there in the dugout.

Earlier in the season, I had asked each player who had signed a release form to prepare a personal bio for me as well. The next week Curtis brought his to me, though only a few did, and in it he said that so far the happiest day he had ever spent was that Saturday when he and Katie kept score of a ball game.

That same day Curtis gave me his bio he told me about meeting a

California appeals court justice. It happened when a number of high court judges were touring the prison. Curtis, due to his pleasant demeanor, intelligence, good manners, and trustworthiness, is often asked to speak to groups of visitors. This has gone on for years. At one point he had a chance to tell the judges about how he was sentenced under the three strikes law. Almost anyone who knows the facts about Curtis' case winces upon hearing the details. It's clear that the sentence he received was far out of proportion to the nature of the crimes—petty theft, a burglary, no violence, no weapons, just stuff that a small-time drug addict gets into. The sentence amounts to fifty years.

I am not political, but even I figure Curtis got a bad deal. So did the justice who actually spoke to Curtis about it and promised to try to do something about it.

Hope had re-entered Curtis's life, and I did not want to shatter that or bring any kind of cloud upon it. Maybe a false hope is better than no hope; maybe it would be enough to get him past the dark depression that had descended upon him. Though not sure, I said nothing negative.

Before the conversation concluded, Curtis asked if he could report, just in case he might be able to get out of prison that he had someplace to go to, a place to live, and a job to work at. He got a quick yes from me. I would take care of that to be best of my ability. And I will; I hope I get the chance.

23

Over Familiarity

Anyone who has read this far might conclude that I have been overly familiar with some of the convicts at San Quentin. If such an observation, or accusation, were made, I would have to agree with it; according to all I have heard in the volunteer meetings, I have at least approached being too personally involved with inmates.

The count I just took in my head runs to over a dozen convicts. There has been nothing sexual, no contraband substances or items brought in,[1] nothing of a personal nature, but rather bonds of various types, even friendships, have been established; it cannot be helped or avoided.

This is the nature of team sports. I have played on and managed baseball teams for fifty-two years now, and it never fails that there will be an inner core, maybe not extending to all, but a core of people with whom bonds of friendship develop. It is part of the game. A team sport is defined by not doing it alone; you are dependent on others. Winning as well as losing contribute to the bonding process. Sports are emotional to the extreme, and the ups and downs can be dramatic. This has been especially true in San Quentin.

Every game is an event, an experience. In North Block and in H Unit, the players will talk endlessly about the games and all that was part of it. Nothing is too insignificant not to be examined minutely. There are few secrets among team members, especially in a prison environment. There is no place to hide; it will come out, and in that place of vulnerability, bonds of friendship will form.

What will I remember ten years from now? I know it will be the players, the coaches, the opposing players, too, but it will not be the scores of

---

1   Coaches will bring in certain items like cups for catchers, a pair of cleats for someone with either really small or large feet, maybe a glove (2 players on the Giants are currently using my gloves and will likely have to keep them, since I won't be able to pick them up), and other items related strictly to baseball equipment needs.

games or batting averages. No, it will be the people, the winning and losing, the pain and frustration, the loves and the hates. Here was life and a touch of freedom. Here was a chance to be a kid again, innocent, and happy having fun.

When I think about my days at the prison I will remember the people—Pete, Bilal, Marcus, Red, Johnny, Curtis, Doug, Frankie, Terry, Stafont, Mike, Chuck, and a host of others. I will think of Kevin, Elliot, Mike, and Stan—my dear friends. And I will think of Chaplain Earl Smith, who along with Leonard, Jimbo, Jason, and Tim got the whole program going. Then there is Don DeNevi who stuck with me through it all, the state employee who was my immediate supervisor. Wow, did we have a time of it. Boys of summer, we did it together!

24
Rage, Anger, and Hate

There are three related emotions, like bosom buddies, without which some would go insane. Some consider them as indispensable friends. Some of those who rely on them are living out their lives in prison.

Two of them play on the A's, and I have become the focus of the evil that is within them. Bobby was present when someone was killed and received a long sentence due to the felony-murder rule. It was a drug deal gone bad, a not unfamiliar circumstance. He heard the judge sentence him to twenty-five to life when he was eighteen. Now thirty-two and with another eleven years before he can be considered for parole, he will spend at least his twenties and thirties with Bubba and the boys. No girlfriend, no wife, no kids, no job, no friends, no nothing, and not much chance this will ever change. Rage, anger, and hate—these are the only friends he has.

Joe is in the same hell hole, except he is a three-striker and with a longer sentence. I'm not sure what the strikes were, since he never talks about the crime, but at age forty-five he could easily do another twenty years. Again, no wife, no kids, maybe a boyfriend, but nothing anyone would want to lay claim to. He lives with rage, anger, and hate.

Frankly, I do not feel bad for either of them; few would want them back on the streets.

Bobby and Joe have embraced their friends and have found someone to share them with—me—which is far safer than other alternatives like the guards or other inmates. You can get written up, a 115, and have more years added to your sentence or even be moved to another prison. It is this last possibility that keeps a lot of cons from losing control completely. San Quentin is a desired home, close to lawyers and courts, and outside visitors come into the prison seven days a week with a myriad of programs, one being baseball.

Neither of the men are big tough guys; and few other cons, including A's players, identify with them. When I ask for a reason for the power Bobby and Joe seem to have I am told they are in tight with the "white boys." I am not convinced of the truth of that. Based on what I have experienced over the years, I think I have become a convenient target for venting their anger and frustration.

Why me? There are reasons, among which are that I have a big, sometimes loud mouth; sometimes I am too belligerent and unyielding, and sometimes my efforts to bring correction and discipline to those I think need it are not appreciated. Apparently, I have developed a bad reputation among some convicts. I have been dumped into the category of a bad cop. This has gone on for years, but Bobby and Joe have played the con with precision this year. One thing for sure, I am not perfect, and I can be a real asshole—I admit it. Nothing new.

I saw it last year. There was a rumor I was a racist. It did not get very far because of the fairly even numbers of the races on the Giants. This year the rumor got more traction, as I was accused of reverse racism. As it happened, there were only two whites on the Giants, and no Hispanics or Pacific Islanders, so it was racism of a different variety. This was dangerous and was maybe why a kite was dropped saying that I was going to be killed. A "kite" may be written or whispered, but it gets to a correctional officer who is then bound to report it. Next I get a call from the investigative unit saying I can no longer come into the prison. The season is nearly over and I still cannot come back in.

The cops in charge of investigations started interviewing inmates, and the accusations mushroomed to the point that my volunteer card was pulled. I am effectively barred from returning for the rest of the year.

Just before the kite was dropped, I made an appointment with a higher-up type in the warden's office who assured me that the rumors I was hearing would be dealt with and speedily. He told me, "You have nothing to worry about."

I am still not sure what happened, but two days after the talk I had with the higher-up, the kite was communicated, and here I sit, writing this. It may be as close as I will get to the team and the game I love, at least this year. I may never get back.

Rage, anger, and hate must go somewhere, either inward or outward. Now I have to deal with these myself. They are not friends; I don't want them, that is clear. Knowing this is not helping right now. In fact, it is plain that I am not fairing so well.

25

The Coaches' Speeches

Monday, July 18, would turn out to be my last day at the prison, certainly for the season, and maybe forever.

The death threat had yet to be dropped. The one on Chris Marshall was found on the floor at PIA where he works; the one on me, I will likely never know.

Saturday, July 9, was when the event happened that necessitated I do something. The Giants were playing a team from the Stockton area, and Kevin was running the game that day. Frankie Smith, our inmate coach, was in the first base coaching box while I was mostly in the dugout. Frankie had to leave the game to attend a class and asked me to go to first base to coach, which I did, and apparently no one saw the change. There I was in the bottom of the seventh when I heard my name being used. It was Bobby and Joe on the other side of the fence that separated the third base visitor's dugout from the area where the convicts, or fans, were. Bobby, with arms waving wildly, was shouting to the opposing team's coaches. It was so loud that even with my poor hearing I could make out that I was being called an asshole, among other honorific titles, and was accused of being bi-polar. I just stood there and listened.

After the inning was over, I had to walk in front of the place where it was still going on and Bobby and Joe saw me. The coach of the visiting team stopped me on my way back to the third base dugout and proceeded to tell me what he had just heard. I explained that I knew because I heard the entire harangue. Bobby and Joe knew they had been observed, and when they walked near me later in the game Bobby pointed his finger at me in simulation of someone shooting a gun and smiled at me. I acknowledged his gesture by slowly shaking my head as though I was saying, "I saw and that was not good."

That next Monday, July 11, I spent an hour in the building that housed the warden's office confiding and asking for counsel from a higher-up. He vowed he would get to the bottom of it and asked me to check back in with him on Thursday. With some vague trepidation, I made the call, and the higher-up's report bothered me; there would be no discipline, nothing. Despite this, I was assured I would be fine. Then the death threat came, which meant there would be an investigation.

Then the practice on Monday the 18th. As usual, the east gate officer did not let us in until 5:30pm. Year after year we would be let in when count cleared, usually some time around 4:39pm. That count is one of many taken throughout the day, but this one demanded that each person be visually counted, which is consistent with every prison in the state. A bell, an old-fashioned bell that hung from a steel frame high above the gateway into the actual prison, would ring six, seven, or more times. It signaled the start of the count. Always at 4pm.

Stan, Mike, and I would sit on a bench in front of the hobby shop store. During the rare times it was open, visitors and members of convicts' families could buy crafts and artwork that the convicts had made. An inmate from the "Ranch" served as the store keeper. The Ranch was a place in the western most part of the sprawling prison, a dorm-like setup, where guys with a low number would spend some time transitioning before going home.[1]

We would sit then and talk, tell stories, and sometimes wave at or converse with the guy who mans the US Post Office just across the street that serves the tiny population of San Quentin Village and the prison itself. About 4:30pm, when all the inmates are found, we will hear the count bell ring, although it is about 130 yards away. At that point one of us will walk to the iron gate and try to catch the eye of the officer. Sometimes there is a response, sometimes not. You get the idea that the guard officer does not care much how long you wait. But if an eye is caught and it would be awkward for the officer to be silent, the word is, "Yeah, let you in at 5." If asked,

---

1   Generally, that are four levels for an inmate, numbered 4 to 1. A point system determines the level. Upon entry to a prison, a convict most often is a #4 level prisoner. Level 4 prisoners go to newer facilities like High Desert, Pelican Bay, Corcoran, and others, where the more dangerous cons can be better controlled. As time goes by, if there are no incidents, the points are lowered, little by little. Being married helps lower points, taking classes, being in drug or alcohol programs, these and other activities help lower points. San Quentin's general population is comprised of level 2 convicts, but guys at the Ranch, or in H Unit, will often have worked the numbers down to level 1. The CDCR, California Department of Corrections and Rehabilitation is quite sophisticated in their evaluation process, and significant incentives to change, at least temporary change, is built into the system.

"Why so late?" the answer, if there was one, would be "warden's office rules."

On game days the opposing teams show up at 4:30pm, overly early, since we can't go in until 5pm, but it takes time for the players to get dressed, go through their equipment bags to make sure nothing unusual is hiding therein, be sure they have their photo ID, sign the visitors sheet, then wait and wait.

Once 5pm rolls around, Stan begins bringing the team in. I have gone in as soon as I am able, before the outside team comes in, in order to get things going down in the lower yard.

Stan works wonders, and without him I would not be any longer involved with the prison. He is like a big brother to me. It is a job to keep me out of trouble, stopping me from doing dumb things, and soothing the feelings of those who are mad at me. Stan gives new teams a lecture and warns, advises, even threatens. The main rule is: nothing in/nothing out and that includes the exchange of any contact info like phone numbers and email addresses. Despite Stan's speech, bad intentions or stupidity will rear their ugly heads.

It is a long walk from the east gate to the count gate, which is the real entrance into the prison. Here the count gate officer, and I am told the higher-ups pick the most cantankerous cops they can find for that duty, collects each player's photo ID and once again runs the info through the computer's list of who has been cleared to come in. On one occasion or another I have mentioned that the east gate officer already ran the names but it never got me anywhere. Then each player's equipment bag is checked, an infra-red stamp is placed on the left wrist, and the sally port's foyer is entered. After the whole team makes it through the count gate, an officer who is seated at a kind of control panel behind a glassed-in portion that extends into the sally port, hits a switch, and a large black iron gate opens, and the players file into the sally port. One by one each person must face the officer in the control room and hold up the photo ID, so the officer can match the actual face with the photo on the ID.

When that is completed, the other end of the sally port's gate opens up, and the guys walk through an entrance into the prison proper. On the left are the chapels, first the Catholic, then the Protestant, then the chapel shared by the Jews and Muslims (ironic in a way), and then by the American Indian chief's office.[2]

---

2   It is not uncommon on Saturday mornings to hear the sound of tom-toms being banged, see smoke arising from the fires that heat up the stones used in the

On the left is the adjustment center, a prison within a prison, where those who have received a death sentence come to adjust to the fact they will not leave the prison alive. Now it is more common for cons to die of disease or old age than be executed.[3]

Four Post, a building about 1,500 square feet, oddly shaped, sits just to the end of the adjustment center and right in front of the new hospital. Here are the officers who monitor who comes in and who goes out. I make it a point to wave at them, but usually I actually stop in and say hello. Some of my favorite officers have been assigned to Four Post.

Then we take a sharp right hand turn, past the hospital, toward cardiac hill and the descent into the lower yard. At the right hand front edge of the hospital, at the top of the hill, is a large black iron door that looks like it came from a medieval castle's front gate. I have never been through the door but have been told that the door was spared from destruction when the new hospital went up, because it marks the location of the prison's first dungeon, and later on, morgue. Stan loves to tell the story to new teams coming in.

Then there is the lower yard. Around the perimeter of the field are steel tables, pull-up bars—space for the different races and they are strictly segregated, too. I do not pass through even the white areas without permission, which is nothing more than a glance at the con who is keeping watch for the group and receiving a favorable nod of the head.

The Pacific Islanders (Hawaiians, Samoans, Vietnamese, Laotians, and so on) have the space to the left of home plate, the whites are in the outfield in the area that runs from right to center fields (which makes it interesting when balls are hit into those areas), the blacks occupy the area around the basketball court (it is the largest of the groups), and the Hispanics are

---

heat up the sweat lodge, and observe naked Indians walking around the encampment that serves as the chapel for the American Indian religion. All this can be seen behind the fence in right-center field.

3 Capital punishment is problematic for me. Sometimes I have thought I would rather die than live a wasted life in a little cell. At other times I have thought that life itself was enough to have despite the conditions. I waffle here, but I think if I had my way I would prefer life without possibility of parole over execution. Where there is life there is hope, and even for the worst of the worse, life is better than death. Without exception, every time that an execution day comes around, I feel somehow complicit or involved, even as just a citizen and voter. Whenever I am around an argument around the subject, I simply listen and contribute little or nothing. I am not convinced that a victim's family really experiences "closure" with the death of a perpetrator, but this is commonly stated.

grouped around the tennis court, which stretches alongside the left field line but close to third base. Those without a group to be part of, and there are such, must find other spaces and often just walk and walk.

Monday now, the 18th, a practice day for the Giants. I had asked each of the coaches to come to it, since we had something to talk over. Kevin Loughlin, Stan Damas, Elliot Smith, Mike Deeble, and I gathered up in left field, while the players were getting ready for the practice. I explained what was up, some of which they were aware of, and we quietly talked among ourselves for some time. We had lost Red and Johnny, it looked like only ten players were healthy enough to play, and I said it may be the last time I would be with the team, this year for sure, and maybe forever.

Now they knew. Sighs and groans, sad faces, a hand on the shoulder but few words. Next, I waved the players over so I could tell them, too. Here were the guys I had been with in the battle that is baseball for several years; some had become friends, and in ways that I am not completely sure of, people I had come to love and care for. In as few words as possible, I explained the circumstances. Then, and it was not expected or planned, one by one the coaches made statements about how they felt. First it was Kevin, then Mike, then Stan. Elliot went last and gave a speech I wish I had recorded. A lawyer in the City, he spoke directly and matter-of-factly, said that he did not always agree with me but that is baseball. He talked about the need to finish the baseball season with dignity and not enter into talk and behavior that would tarnish them as Giants. Yes, it would be tempting to blame some of the A's players, but that must not happen.

Speeches now given and finished, we turned and walked toward the dugout. I picked up my equipment bag and said that I was going home. Slowly and silently, the guys came up and gave me a hug, told me they loved me—yes the cons did use the word—and they hoped I would be back soon.

Slowly walking up cardiac hill with the thought in my mind that it would be for the last time, I thought back to that day in 2010 when we all said good-bye to Chris Rich. Just at the point where I would no longer be visible to the guys on the field, I had turned around and waved my hand, and looking up at me from about 100 yards away, Chris returned my wave. Once again I did the same, waved, and a bunch of Giants waved back.

San Quentin Baseball

Photos

Note: To See any of these photos and many more in color, go to ww.flickr.com/photos/earthenvesselnet/

1998 Pirates - Coaches and Captains

1998 Pirates - Team and Coaches

2001 Giants Team

2007 Giants Team

2008 Giants Team

2009: Four Coaches: Kevin, Len, Stan, Kent

2010 Color Guard Seen through Fence

2010 Kent Watching a Fly Ball

2011 Giants and A's Teams

2011 Bill Rodriques, CDW

2011 Catcher Johnny Taylor and Kent

2011 High Fives at End of Game

2011 James Bautista before the "Fans"

2011 Ke Lam Pitching

2011 Kent and Lt. Robinson

2011 Kevin Driscoll Batting

2011 Kevin Driscoll Pitching

2011 Kevin Loughlin, Coach

2011 Lt. Robinson, an A's Fan

2011 Mike Deeble, Coach

2011 Pregame Coaches Meeting

2011 Red Casey in the Twilight Zone

2011 Sliding into Home

2011 Stan Damas, Coach

2011 Vern Philpott, Flag Football Coach

2011 Santa Monica Suns Team

26
2012 Preface

Panic Attack

It must have been somewhere in 1993 or 1994 that I learned the destructive force of anxiety.

Prior to my involvement in the baseball program, I was part of a ministry outreach begun by Chaplain Earl Smith and Carl Gleeman. Earl was the chaplain of the Protestant chapel, and together with Carl he developed a cell-to-cell visitation program. I started with it in 1986 and came into the prison every Thursday evening to go to the blocks and talk to the inmates in their cells. We would distribute Bibles and other Christian literature as we endured the thick cigarette smoke and clamor of voices that was a normal part of life in the five-tier blocks.

Sometimes we were in North Block, other times in West Block, rarely in South Block with its four divisions of Alpine, Badger, Carson, and Donner. The time I have in mind, I was in West Block. We never went into East Block with its overflow from Condemned Row and segregation cells. The "Row" was mostly in North Block, a kind of sixth tier that was not visible if inside North Block; once the row was full, East Block was used for the condemned prisoners.

It was not a pleasant winter's night, and I ended up going alone to West Block. This is where new convicts would be housed soon after arrival, and often I found some who still had on ordinary street attire. The guys, most in orange jumpsuits, had been fed and were all locked down in their cells. At the time, there was only one man per cell, and the wire mesh had yet to go up over the bars.[1]

---

1   The mesh was meant to prevent attacks on the officers or other inmates who happened along. Some cons knew how to turn toilet paper rolls and the paper itself into spears. Urine and feces would be collected and thrown into the faces of officers—not very pleasant, and this was in the day when anyone of the inmates

Entering the block, I stood for a moment to look and listen. The concrete and steel acted almost like a megaphone, and the noise was almost overwhelming. It was far louder than anything I had experienced in any other block.[2]

Amidst the myriad of voices, I could hear someone yelling out, "I was not supposed to be here. This is a mistake. Get me out of here. I don't belong here!" Desperate, scared, panicked—these and more were evident in the pleadings—and I knew no one would be paying attention.

The voice seemed to be up on the third tier, so I climbed the steel stairwell and followed the ongoing protestations until I came face to face with the subject.

White, middle-aged, no tattoos in evidence, no piercings; he looked like a regular guy with family and a job, some education, someone who lived the average American life. When he saw me, a visible sigh of relief came from him and he fell at his knees almost ready to worship me. We shook hands, exchanged names, and in a rush or words he let me know how it was that the whole thing was a mistake.

I have told the story so often, the details are yet assessable to my mind. He was in for what might be called a white collar crime, which I think was fraud or theft, but on a large scale. No priors, never involved with the criminal justice system, and he left at home a wife and some kids. He lost everything he had gained, the house would be sold, and it would be five or more years before he would be free.

Anxiety is a powerful emotional/mental condition and is common to us all. I figured out I was prone to it when I was fifteen years old, and it was a contributing factor to my focus on psychology in college.[3]

Anxiety, if untreated, can quickly move into dangerous territory. As I understand it, there are two kinds of anxiety: One, the anxiety of feeling trapped, that something has happened or is going to happen, and, two, separation anxiety or abandonment anxiety. Here then is this guy who got greedy, wanted more than his share, and something awful had happened

---

might be HIV positive. With the mesh, things were safer but it blocked out most of the already dull light from penetrating into the cells.

2   The cons in North Block would not tolerate the yelling and cacophony characteristic of the other blocks. North Block was for mainliners only, and they wanted to live quiet and peaceful lives, as best they could.

3   During the 1970s I operated the Marin Christian Counseling Center in San Rafael. I was the only counselor and did not charge for my services. I was an unlicensed counselor and advertised it as "pastoral counseling."

with more likely to happen, things that he could not even get his mind to explore, and he was separated from all that he loved and felt comfortable with.

Right in front of me he was having a panic attack, and no one would or could do anything about it. In fact, he might get beaten up by officers or other cons if he did not bring it under control. In time, after some months, he might get some meds prescribed, a pill to calm him down, but that was only a maybe.

The panic he experienced, if left untreated, might usher him into deeper trouble, maybe into a full-blown psychosis. That guy was well on his way, and likely, in the years in the brutal environment that was and is San Quentin, he might never recover.

Now, what does this have to do with baseball in SQ? The answer is integral to the story that follows and the stories that went before. These are the ball players down on the field. To one degree or another they have experienced the damaging impact of uncontrolled anxiety, even Post Traumatic Stress Disorder, which belongs in the anxiety category. And I knew from day one in 1997 when I started working with the guys on the baseball team, that at least some of them would be struggling with diminished ability to cope with the real world.

By the way, I am not fixing blame; we have what we have, and if we, meaning our society, even understood the dynamics of it all and at the same time had the means to deal with it, probably even then the problem would be running wild. We are all subject to the vicissitudes of the human condition. Prison is an attempt to mollify it at least to some degree.

27
2012 Introduction

The Giants ended the 2011 season with 14 wins, 12 losses, and 1 tie. We played some good teams, and among them were two community college teams. We did amazingly well.

In June of 2011, a rumor was floated around the yard that I was a reverse racist. Apparently the "white boys" were responsible for this. Now for the third time I have been accused of racism, but this is the first time for favoring the Blacks. The rumor was followed by a death threat, and as I learned later it came from one of the white boys, so I missed the last month of the season—my volunteer card was pulled. Death threats are not always death threats. they are really just ways to force a non-convict out of the prison. It is a manipulative tactic that inmates know how to employ.

Convicts have power. For instance, a female teacher at the prison's education department gave one nutty guy an F grade, and he proceeded to drop a "kite" (insider word for a death threat) on her. She signed a waver saying she understood the threat against her and wanted to continue anyway. But by the time the third threat was dropped, she had become an emotional wreck and was forced to leave the prison. I expect to incur a series of threats, yet I will continue as long as I can.

Kites are dropped in one of the mailboxes—there is at least one in each cell block for the cons to send letters out. The investigative unit has few options other than removing the subject of the threat from the prison.

West Block

After five-and-one-half months, I finally got back into the prison, not for baseball, but to be with my son Vernon, who had taken over the flag football team in 2010. West Block, which had formally housed prisoners going through classification, challenged North Block to a football game. West Block had gone main-line or general population before the end of 2011. Previously, the block had housed cons newly arrived into the prison system who were going through classification to determine which prison should take them. Eight hundred new inmates are now housed in West Block, most of whom are young, aggressive, and restless. And numerous of them want to play baseball. And I saw this personally when Vern and I were at the prison to oversee the football game. In intensity and fan involvement, it reminded me of a Raiders or 49ers game.

The change that has come to the prison with the new West Block is due to the fact that most of them are level 3 prisoners. There are, in general, four levels of custody. Four is the highest level, one the lowest. Four means high custody, one would be low security or custody level. The new West Block inmates were level three, but with the stroke of an administrative pen, due to budget cuts, could be made level two. North Block and H Unit are filled with level two inmates. And there is significant difference between two and three.

A Football game—North Block versus West Block

The game was played January 21. Vern and I got there right on time, 9am, but there was not a convict on the yard. An officer approached us and said there was a problem with the chow hall, and the yard would not be open until 10am. So, we walked, talked, and waited. At the hour the yard filled with more cons than I had ever seen before—the impact of West Block. The North Block team came out, stretched, ran, and got suited up for the eight-man flag football game. Vern and I had placed the cones on the field marking the boundaries and yard markers, so we were set, but there was no West Block team. Everyone was milling around grumbling about the no-shows, when all of a sudden, we heard a loud roar and running onto the field, from the direction of the basketball court, was the team, the new team, and they had gotten their West Block guys to form a kind of tunnel for them to run through. Here they came, fast, loud, and gesturing signs I did not understand, and they gathered to the center of the field and started chanting, the kind you might hear at a Stanford or Cal game. West Block had arrived.

The game was close right up to the very end, then with a minute left, the new guys scored the winning touchdown, and they went wild. The North Block guys were stunned, but when they recovered, they did not hesitate to congratulate their opponents. Vern and I were put on notice, however, that we had entered a new era at the prison.[1]

Plan B

During the game I was besieged by cons from both of the blocks.

---

1 On Wednesday, February 9, there was a riot among the West Block prisoners. The San Francisco Chronicle's headline was, "4 inmates badly injured during riot in exercise yard." (SF Chronicle, 2-10-12, p. C2.) The riot took place, not on the Lower Yard, but in the concrete yard hard by West Block. Likely it was a turf determining sort of thing—who controlled the drugs, sex, and prime hangout space.

(There are other blocks, East and South, but the inmates there are not main line and do not come onto the lower yard.) Everyone, almost entirely guys who had played for the A's and the new West Block guys, wanted to know what was going to happen with the baseball season. I was somewhat shocked to find that they knew about as much about the details of the new season, Plan B, (see below) as I did. The reason I was not more shocked than I was is because I knew there was cell phone communications going on, and that is as detailed as I can get about that right now.

One thing was obvious, the pleasant time of playing baseball, running around on the green grass, and enjoying the sunny days—this was not going to happen for yet another year. It would be months of struggle, at minimum, and I again began to question whether my son and I should be there at all.

Plan B we are calling it. It severely shuffles the deck; the Giants and the A's will be broken up with a draft. Some guys have a lot to lose. The white boy's network will be dismantled, at least to some degree, and some of the players from last year will be fortunate to make a team, given the abundance of new talent in West Block.

To be able to play baseball at San Quentin is a highly sought after privilege. Wearing a uniform that once was worn by an actual major league ball player is one thing, then there is the media attention, and the team and individual photos players get after the season is over. And those photos, which I have been supplying for years now, are a really big deal. I post many of these online at flickr which can be viewed by going to www.flickr.com and typing in San Quentin or Kent Philpott.

Plan B effectively doubles the number of cons playing baseball. There will be the A's, the Giants, and two minor teams, maybe named the Dodgers and Angels. With twelve inmate coaches, three per team, the total runs to eighty involved in the baseball program. It scares the liver out of me, handling all the egos and the mentals, who usually would be locked up in facilities where they can be more closely monitored. But now with the budget problems facing California, the crowding is worse and the correctional officers far fewer. One guard told me recently, "You are going to be on your own." Hope he was exaggerating.

I am told that the West Block guys are not like the North Block guys who are mostly older, lifers, more mellow folks who just want to live out their lives as peacefully as possible. The West Block guys are younger, more violent, and pushy. Many have little to lose and are ready to do battle with whomever they can. And the gang presence is huge now; I am told this by officers and inmates alike.

28

More Death Threats

Thursday, March 15, 2012

Plan B is no more. Now there will only be two teams, mostly due to a few guys who played for the A's in 2011. They did not want a draft, because, as I have heard, they were afraid they would not be chosen in the draft.

These disgruntled ones were in regular contact, by means of smuggled cell phones, with two of their coaches who got way too close to the convicts, something called over-familiarity. (This charge is based on bits of evidence that have come to me since May of 2011, but it is not completely determined that the cons did indeed have access to a cell phone.)[1] Together they conspired to keep things as they were last season with the draft only filling in if and when needed.

The bottom line, however, is that I am responsible for the problem, since I was the one who brought these guys in to coach the A's in the first place. These two did not function as head coaches but were assistants. The head coach, another guy I was responsible for bringing in, did not run the team at all but left that work to a convict. It was a strange mix: two assistant coaches put themselves into the game, and a convict made out the lineups and the calls at the third base coaching box.

The baseball program became more and more popular, and the need for a second team was obvious. For that to happen, more coaches were needed. I had no idea they would get caught up in the game cons love

---

1 In 2011 the prison conducted a sweep of North Block aimed at finding cell phones. Three hundred phones were found, 200 outside the block scattered around the upper yard and another 100 in cells. That means that one third of the convicts in North Block had a cell phone. Cell phones fetch as much as $500 so there is a steady supply. How do they get in? A phone call, a letter, all coded per plan, says how much money for what contraband item is to taken to the person who will bring the item(s) in. Once done, the outside outlaws have a power hold on the person who broke the law, thus insuring compliance.

to play—making "ducks" out of free people, whether volunteers or state employees. You make a duck, so you can you-know-what, and that is what happened to the new coaches. The central dynamic is an exploitation of a desire to be liked by the convicts.

Prison is boring to the extreme, and to create some excitement or to find a way to manipulate things, con games are continuously run. The fun part for the prisoners is to spend huge amounts of time plotting the strategy. It is like a chess game played on a large scale. I don't judge it one way or another, as I might well do the same given the same circumstances. But it can be dangerous for those who are being manipulated.

Rumors are key to the cons' fun. An inmate might start a rumor in the morning and then check on its progress at the end of the day, just to see how it had morphed. Rumors that get a lot of traction have to do with who is coming in and who is going out. The rumor that impacted me most was the one wherein I was going to be kicked out of the prison.

The plot only partially succeeded. Things were swinging in my favor, when all of a sudden, I got a call from a sergeant at the prison's Investigative Unit who read to me three death threats that had been deposited in the box into which the prisoners place their outgoing mail. Actually, only two were real threats. One read in part, "There is a hit contract out on our dear coach and we want him protected." There followed the usual questioning of the usual suspects, who were read the riot act, and that was it. Of course, I get only the briefest of details, but more will probably be forthcoming once I make it back down to the lower yard.

That was last Wednesday, the 7th of March, and already things have cleared up, and I am once again allowed to go back in.

The threats do not much comfort the other coaches. Surprisingly, however, I have been able to add three new coaches to our staff this year, one being my son Vernon, who was a Desert Storm war vet, a military policeman, and is not easily frightened.

There will be a draft, which is set for next week, March the 24th, and it will then become apparent who will prevail.

I have a suspicion and hope I am not going paranoid here, but I have a rather strong sense of things that the "white boys" have somehow gotten the ear of the powers that be, really one person whom I cannot identify. But if I am right, what is left of Plan B will be trashed, and the same old set-up as last year—that miserable, stressful year—will be in place once again. At this point, I am not clear how I will proceed, if my worst fears are realized, but I will not quit no matter what. I refuse to let my enemies get the better of the situation.

I am determined not to get angry and start saying stupid things like I have in the past. Seems like every careless word I have spoken was remembered, twisted, and used against me. Sometimes I lose it on the yard; I know better but can't seem to stem the flow of scandalous words. I will talk way too harshly to convicts. Maybe I try too hard to live up to what has long been said of me by those who know me best: "Philpott takes no shit."

29

First Day of Tryouts

March 24 or maybe March 31

After a week's worth of rain, which knocked out what was to be the first day of tryouts, it looked like we were finally going to conduct our first tryout on March 24. But then a seagull flew into a power line.

The prison went dark, that early March night. And it was a dark and stormy winter's night already. No lights at a prison! Worst case scenario indeed. Just after I had contacted all the coaches, the call came in from Don about how a huge generator was going to be installed at the prison on the 24th, and all programs were to be cancelled. Right away, my worry-wart brain began to fear that opening day would arrive, and we would not be ready.

March 31 did roll around. Saturday morning on the lower yard with a full contingent of coaches, including two I wish were no longer with the baseball program, and a bunch of eager, excited convicts, all of whom wanted to impress the coaches with how good they were at baseball.

I figured there would be a move made by a couple of coaches to sabotage the draft process, and for some weeks I pulled as many strings as I could to prevent that from happening. It should never have come to this, but now the only thing to do is go on. For the first time, in a serious way, I wanted to walk away from it all. Now at age seventy, I find it difficult to fight the battles, but this one I was going to deal with. I knew another threat or an incident of almost any kind could end the baseball program. One powerful person at the prison told me he was looking for any excuse to shut us down.

My good friend, Don DeNevi, the state employee who has overseen the baseball program for the past twelve years, has helped me ensure that Plan B would move forward, even though there would be two teams and instead of four. We talk on the phone often and do what is within our power to have a recreational program that works for the inmates. Without Don being of the same mind as I am, I would have walked away long ago. But we have consistently supported each other.

Don cannot take the same stand as I do against those who would bend the baseball program to suit their own agenda. By "those" I mean the several inmates that started the trouble as players for the A's last year and those two A's coaches who became their ducks.

Don and I agree that the inmates are acting out of the fear that they will be left out, not drafted, since there are the new guys on the Block—much younger and apparently quite talented as athletes. Now, we can empathize with that, but we are not giving in to it either. The program demands an equal and fair chance for a convict to make one of the teams, and the draft is our solution. And that is the whole deal—a process of selecting players based on their baseball skills and not on a good ole boys' agreement.

30

Opening Day

The San Rafael Pacifics and the U.S. Military Baseball Team

Opening days—May 26 and August 18—will be very special dates for the San Quentin baseball teams, both for the Giants and the A's.

On May 26, the San Rafael Pacifics, a professional baseball team, will be playing a game at the prison. The former Dodger power hitter and right fielder from the 1980s, Mike Marshall, will be up against an all-star team from the A's and Giants on Opening Day.

Everyone is justifiably excited about it. Scads of media will be on the field recording just about everything possible. I anticipate that it will mean a lot to both teams.

At first, Mike Marshall, or as he signs his emails, MM, and I thought about switching batteries. That is, their pitcher and catcher would play for the prison team, and our pitcher and catcher would play for the Pacifics. After thinking it over, it seemed better to just try our best to beat those guys.

Prior to that, on May 19, Elliot Smith's team, the Oaks/Cubs, will be in Saturday morning for an opening day prior to the real opening day on the 26th. That evening the A's and Giants will play each other for the purpose of determining the "all stars" that will go up against the San Rafael Pacifics.

The Red, White, and Blue Tour

Around the middle of February, I began getting emails from a Terry Alvord, who I thought was a manager of a local adult men's baseball team that wanted to come in and play a game at the prison. Since it was way too early to schedule any games, I merely read the email and replied that the scheduling would take place toward the last of March. That was followed by a couple more emails from Terry, and I happened to open up an attachment to one of them. I was shocked at what I saw.

To my surprise, his team is the U.S Military Baseball Team, on what they called the Red, White, and Blue Tour to raise money for wounded war veterans. They were heading up north from southern California and intending to go up through Oregon and Washington and then into Canada. They wanted to make a stop at the prison and play the team. But that was not all.

Looking at the few photos attached I was startled to notice that some of the players had metal legs. The players themselves were wounded vets. Our teams, and it is teams plural, are going to play them on August 18, one in the morning, the other in the evening. In the middle of the day, they want to connect with local VFW chapters. Then the next day, Sunday, the team will visit our little Miller Avenue Baptist Church in Mill Valley, where I am pastor. We will have a breakfast for them, then they will take over the service and preach and teach, then we will have lunch for them before they head out up north in their bus. What an honor!

My son Vern was in Desert Storm, and I consider him a real war hero. I served as a medic for four years with the Air Force. So, it is a good match, and we are privileged to be involved in this.

There will be lots of media at this game, too. Cameras do funny things to people, me included. Looking at a camera, we will do and say stupid things we later wish we hadn't. I am especially concerned about convicts with agendas who like to take advantage of situations. This stuff is out of my control, so I just have to let it go. However, I will have a little talk about proprieties with the coaches and the players.

Wow, the Red, White, and Blue Tour—I wonder how the cons might get involved in the fund raising?

31

Scheduling

The worst part of this job is filling out the game schedule for the teams. It is almost full-time job—at least you could make into one, if you were neurotic enough. (I just barely escape.)

After being contacted by an outside team who want to come in, I send them an email with the schedule along with a gate clearance form and a little piece I wrote titled, "Considerations for teams." (It appears at the end of this chapter.)

This is all pretty simple, but the trouble begins with the gate clearance. On the form, four pieces of information are requested for each person coming in: name as on the driver's license; that driver's license number; date of birth; and social security number. A person at the prison, in the warden's office, goes into an FBI data base, which is very sensitive, and the person will either be cleared or denied. If denied, I hope to be told about this to prevent the player from making the effort to come only to be turned away at the East Gate. Sometimes I am so informed; other times I am not.

Where the trouble comes in is when team managers try to get a player or two cleared in mere days ahead of the game date. Usually, a week or more is required.[1] Not that it takes so long to do the clearances, but it is a bureaucratic thing, and there are rules and policies that must be followed.

It is a gamble whether the add-ons will be cleared or not, and in these rush deals, I mostly never know what happened. Now we are at the gate, and the players are all hoping to get in. Driver's licenses are collected then handed to the officer at the East Gate, who disappears into his little shack where he runs the names through his computer. Invariably he will emerge with two piles of licenses; one set that cleared, the other that didn't. The denied players sometimes take it okay, but some do not. There has been many a scene

---

1 San Quentin has bureaucracies galore, and they war with each other. Rules change at a whim, and now a list of gate clearances require to be in a month prior to the date the team is scheduled to come in.

at the gate when the denied person(s) only has me to blame. Though I try to explain what might have happened, the disappointment can run deep. More than once a whole team will actually refuse to come for a game when even one of their players is turned away.

One incident I will not forget easily was when a Marine, just back from Iraq, had only his military I.D. with him, which had his photo on it. The whole team cleared but him. I resolved to get him in, so I headed into the prison to find the watch commander in the Captain's Porch and argue the case. He was not there, but I was told he was in the cafeteria located just east of the Count Gate, the main entrance into the heart of the prison.

The captain was seated having coffee with several other officers of rank, and I excused myself and presented the Marine's I.D. It was examined, and then the watch commander said, "Nope, has to be a driver's license."

A few years ago, a team came up from Los Angeles. They flew up on the Friday before the Saturday game, stayed at a nearby hotel, and there they were, eagerly looking forward to playing a real baseball game in one of the most famous prisons in the world.

The day before, wanting to make sure, I contacted the powers that were responsible for the gate clearances and was told that the whole team was cleared and there were no denials. Armed with that I phoned the manager of the team and said everything was a go.

Not one got in; not one name was on the computer. I visited the watch commander, pleaded and begged, but no, sorry. I gathered the licenses, wrote all the information down on a piece of paper, made out a statement saying I would take full responsibility. Nope, Sorry. I am still upset about it.

Below now is something I developed that I thought might make things go more smoothly for visiting teams.

CONSIDERATIONS FOR TEAMS

1. Please leave valuables in cars, or better yet, at home.
2. Bring a picture ID. Make sure to secure it during the game.
3. No cell phones, cameras, or other electronic devices.
4. A photo of the team may be taken in front of the East Gate before entering into the prison.
5. No blue, grey, orange, or yellow jerseys—convicts wear these colors.
6. Can bring in water in a clear plastic bottle and a snack if necessary.
7. Please do not give an inmate anything at all. "Nothing in, nothing out" is the watchword.

8. We must comply with anything asked by a correctional officer.

9. We cannot make a phone call for or contact anyone for an inmate.

10. No items of clothing may be given to an inmate, including batting gloves, hats, cleats, etc.

11. Conversation may be made with an inmate but be careful not to divulge any personal information. Do not ask a person what crime he committed.

12. You will not be able to visit an inmate at a later date.

13. We have never had an incident of violence; this is not a worry.

14. A number of officers will be watching from various locations, and the whole thing will be video-taped—but you will not be aware of this.

15. Try to ignore inmates who may come up behind the open dugout and want to engage in conversation. Be polite but discreet.

16. The officiating is usually poor, and we hope close calls go for the visitors.

17. It is not uncommon for players, who were supposed to be cleared in, turn out to be denied anyway. There is little or no recourse then. I suggest every player bring along a good book to read and maybe something to eat and drink while waiting for the rest of the team to finish their game. This does not happen often, but it happens and for reasons we do not understand.

18. The whole point is to have fun and play baseball.

Thank you for being willing to come in. For many it is an unforgettable experience.

Kent Philpott

32

Thin Ice

The CDW gathered up the members of the A's and Giants as best he could on the Lower Yard, wherein is The Field of Dreams, and told them I was on "thin ice." This was just after I had received three new death threats. From what I heard, the two cons behind the threats had convinced the CDW that I was largely to blame for the troubles between the two baseball teams. "One more time that Philpott acts in an arrogant, rude, or disrespectful way, and he is gone."

Now how will I proceed? There certainly will be a time when doing nothing more than acting the part of a leader that I will unwittingly provide my enemies with something to tattle to Rodriquez about. A simple decision as a baseball coach during a baseball game, and that could be it.

I figure the CDW got bought by the convicts, persuaded by them, and without talking to me about it at all. All the Giants players, and some A's players as well, who stood by me, apparently did not matter much.

It is now May, and opening day is two weeks away. There have been no tryouts, since the CDW wants to "punish" the cons. One instigator has gone to the hole and is still there,[1] which is a step in the right direction, and rumor has it that he will be transferred to another prison. Rumors are just that, and they are often spread just to see how well they do, a kind of perverse entertainment.

Thin ice—I will certainly fall through that, and I am at the point where I don't care that much about it. More than a decade and a half, and the powers that be could care less. The usual refrain is: "This is a prison, you know." My reply is: "Sure I know I am in a prison, but volunteers should not be treated like convicts." Not that convicts should be mistreated. They are too often abused, and I guess the thugs who run prisons don't know the difference between a prisoner and a volunteer or don't care that there is one.

1   This convict was transferred out of San Quentin during the third week of May, and to where, no one seems to know.

Thugs! Not a complementary label, but I think an accurate one, at least for many who work in prisons. A newly hired correctional officer may have the best of intentions and genuinely want to make a difference. I have talked to them, some who were college grads with degrees in psychology, sociology, criminal justice, and so on, who saw the job as a way to give back or make a difference.

Things change, though, and it may take a few months, maybe a few years. The code of conduct among CO's does not allow for a touchy-feely approach. There is a certain demeanor that is clearly enforced. Then there is the impact of the cons' behavior on the COs. When I talk about this issue with outsiders they are often surprised at this and disbelieving. Prisoners can seem like such wonderful people; they have learned the art of presenting themselves in the best of lights. Without realizing it, people are "turned" and develop an antagonism toward the criminal justice system, which of course is flawed and corrupt like most other human institutions, and they develop a view of the convicts as opponents. It happens every day. The CO who comes in with a clean slate is radicalized without seeing what is happening to him or her and may then become a thug.

Thug behavior is rewarded by the jailers and confirmed by those in jail; it is an example of the proverbial vicious cycle. Abuse begets abuse, and round and round it goes. What matters to the caring young correctional officer is nothing much more than a paycheck with benefits. The ideal for way too many of those who operate our jails and prisons is "lock em up and throw away the key."

It is no real wonder that I am on thin ice. If my volunteer card is pulled and I am forced to walk away from a program I have struggled to build over the years, what price will I pay? How long will it take me to get over it? Will I let my heart get hard?

33

Suspended

Here we sit with no tryouts, unable to schedule games, waiting for the prison officials to finish up their investigation into the death threats and figure out what to do with the troublemakers. Seems like it is simple: to the hole with you, or to Pelican Bay with you. The question comes to me: Why now are certain convicts being coddled?

No answers, week after week. Teams are contacting me, and I am filling out the schedule, but maybe there will be no baseball. Then I get the following email:

> "Please be advised that effective immediately, the San Quentin Recreational Baseball, Softball, and Football programs[1] , and all associated volunteers for those programs, are suspended pending investigation.
>
> "The existing volunteer ID cards and gate clearances have been pulled from the E. Gate. Any pending IDs are being withheld from final processing, until this investigation is complete and the matter resolved."

The new professional baseball team in town, the San Rafael Pacifics, are on the verge of having to forget coming in to play our team. What about the Military Baseball Team? It is probably too late to contact various media now about coming in. The pitchers cannot possibly be ready, even if the suspension were lifted today. It takes two to several months for a pitcher to build up arm strength and be ready to throw for even a few innings.

The CDW has every right to suspend the whole thing. His job is to maintain the integrity of the prison, and seeing to recreational opportunities does not figure high on his priority list. Okay, that is a given. What rights do I have? None, really, and there would not be a blip on the screen should I drop dead this very day.

---

[1] Only the sports programs I am responsible for are suspended.

Just how important is the prison baseball program to me? Have I lost my balance here? Could I take walking away after so many years of struggle? Not to get overly philosophical about this, but life is not fair. Cons, those who do not get very far along the rehabilitation schematic, think life should be fair, but they have seen nothing of fairness, and they are mad as hell, or madder than hell, and no reasonable argument, if one could be made, will suffice.

This whole thing is unfair, and it will likely never be corrected.

34

Barred from the Prison

Today, on June 1, 2012 (not to be overly dramatic but simply to document the event), I was informed that **I am barred from the prison for life**. "Barred" not banned—this is a prison we are talking about. This good news came to me via my son who was so informed by Don. The directive had been issued by the CDW. (The CDW will go unnamed.)

The CDW—I have referred to him as the thug/bully. During three meetings this year in his office I said virtually nothing while he threatened and lectured and bullied me, just like any other thug.

The first meeting with him was the most interesting—the middle of the summer 2011, on an invitation from him. He had told me that if I needed to talk to him I could; I took him up on it. He started off, and there were just the two of us in his very large and nicely appointed office, and he let me know he was the tough prison administrator, swore like crazy, and boasted of how he almost made the L.A. Dodgers, back when.

He did not know I was a Baptist pastor, and when he found out, almost by accident, his language changed to that of a choir boy, and he told me about his involvement in his church. Wow, what a change, but it served as an omen as to his mercurial nature.

So much has happened so quickly, it nearly fries my mind to try to put it in some semblance of order.

I am going to start at the beginning and hit at least the major points.

One, back in July of 2010, due to an inmate, Noe Valdivia, we started what was to be an intramural team made up of guys who hadn't made the Giants. I asked Len Zemarkowitz, who had been coaching with the Giants, to do this. There were some capable players on the team, and Len did a good job in forming it. They thought they were better than the Giants, and after a couple of practice games, they proved they were as good if not better than the Giants. And so, the trouble started.

Two, Noe, a very good jail house lawyer, now out of prison, agitated the powers that be to create a second team, yet without a name, alongside the Giants, which would also play outside teams. This did not set well with me, because I did the scheduling, and that was definitely the worst part of my whole baseball experience at the prison. But it was finally agreed that the new arrangement would begin in 2011.

An early obstacle was that none of the Giants coaches wanted to work with the new team. Looking back, I should have gone over and done it myself, but instead I contacted two baseball guys I knew who had both come into the prison helping out or were members of an outside team—one I will name Bill and the other Larry (not their real names). In they came; we got them brown cards so they could come in unescorted, and the new team started playing ball as the A's. I had contacted the real Oakland A's team, and they graciously supplied us with uniforms, really nice major league uniforms. The no-name team became the A's.

The A's and Giants played four times in 2011, and the Giants won each game, none of which were close. And that only made matters worse.

The first time we played, which was the week before opening day, the trouble started. (I was told by Larry that the trouble had already begun, however.) Bill started an argument with me over a Giants player using a wood bat, just after he got a bloop hit with one. True, the prison had banned wood bats, because an officer had witnessed the shattering of a maple bat, which broke into odd pieces, some of which looked a lot like shives. But the prison had rules, and we had ours, and they did not always coincide. All kinds of bats were being used, but as soon as the Giants got a hit with a wood bat, the fight started.

The first time I said okay, the batter is out. The Giants were already on the board, and the A's were being stopped cold. Larry and I talked it out and finally agreed that wood or metal, any bat was good. Then, toward the end of the game and another single with a wood bat, and it was another argument.

Two A's players and one inmate coach emerged as the primary antagonists. Chris, Jeff, and YaYa. It turned into a kind of war, and I was the enemy—I guess only me, since I was in charge of the program. Don DeNevi had so appointed me, but that would change from time to time, based on how much I did for him and the program.

Then I figured something out. The A's would play or practice on Wednesday nights and the Giants on Thursdays. (Both teams played outside teams on Saturdays.) Bill would either call me or email me on a Friday morning about something that had happened on the previous Thursday night.

It took a few of these to make me wonder how he knew on Friday morning what had happened on Thursday evening, especially since neither he nor Larry had been there.

"Bill," I asked, "how do you know about what happened last night?" Now I have been around some, and I knew by merely talking to him that he was stoned. It had not occurred to him that I might realize there had to have been some communication going on with the cons. Hmmm. Well, that was the last time Bill made that mistake. Fuel had been poured on the flames, and it was not long thereafter that I was accused of reverse racism, since the Giants were mostly black and the A's mostly white.

That was not enough, but the death threat made in late July of 2011 was enough to have me removed from the prison for the rest of the season. I had no recourse, and a death threat was a typical means for a convict to manipulate things. It happens all the time.

So, I was out before the 2012 season even began, and at least four new threats with my name on them were placed in the mail drop box in North Block. The investigative Unit went to work and eventually found out about the cell phones being brought in. It was Bill, and Larry told me that Bill would have to find another way to make some money. If any other contraband was brought in, I am not sure. But I found out that $1,500 worth of pills, meth of course, could fit into a hollowed-out baseball, and about $5,000 worth of marijuana could be stuffed into a first baseman's or catcher's mitt, if most of the stuffing were taken out. Only the Investigative Unit knows for sure whether this really occurred with Bill.

Simple: as the watchdog over the program I became an enemy, a threat to the whole operation. I had to go.

There were meetings with the CDW in his office, and I have to say that he bullied me and played the thug, and I had not one chance to speak to anything.

The process is quite familiar: the whole prison system, however necessary it is, and it is, nevertheless turns otherwise normal people into thugs and bullies on both sides of the bars. I have seen it for thirty years. It is the rare con and the rare guard who does not fall into the pit.

I left behind idealistic notions shortly after I got into the military, and I know the world is not fair, but I always thought I ought to have a chance to speak to the issues. If I screwed up, I would like a chance to apologize, make amends if possible, and make changes if I could do so. The chance never came. I was working on the season from behind the proverbial scene, all the while getting madder and madder. Finally, I vented to Don on the phone and in frustration I said, "I am going to write a letter to Cate."[1] The very next day, I was informed through my son Vernon, whom Don had called, that the CDW got really pissed that I should go to Cate—so "barred from the prison for life."

I resigned then in a formal letter sent to Don, and it is that which you see at the end of this final chapter for the 2012 season. Indeed, I'm going out with a whimper, but out I am. I do not want to go sour grapes, sling accusations, or find ways to retaliate. My time is up; perhaps it should have happened a couple of years ago. Things end, and my time as coach of the San Quentin Giants is over.

---

1   Matthew Cate is the secretary for the California Department of Corrections and Rehabilitation.

35

Just Before the End

Yesterday Captain XX emailed me asking for the baseball equipment back. In the same email I was informed that he and Lt. XXX were taking charge of the program. He also wanted the schedule and the contact info. I emailed back that I would bring the equipment to the East Gate in a few days and that another coach had the schedule and the contact info and provided a way to contact that coach.

The Captain—the once and present public affairs officer for the prison—championed the A's in 2010 and 2011. He was "turned" by two ball players. These two clever cons convinced him that the A's, the underdogs, deserved more; they deserved first class status. Indeed, they sold the idea that the A's were a better team and needed to replace the Giants. The Captain, an A's fan, did what he could to establish the A's on a par, at least, with the Giants. A number of times I would hear, "Well, the Captain is on our side."

My wife Katie formulated a theory last year, 2011, that the prison would like to take the baseball program away from me. Now that the cameras and media folks were showing more and more interest, they wanted the glory, or so she thought. I never overtly agreed but thought that it might be possible. But the Captain always came across as such a gentleman.

Perhaps this conspiracy type theory explains why I was treated as I was. Accused without an opportunity to hear the accusations much less defend myself; verbally abused by ZZZ without a single chance to say a word in reply. Then, on not so much as a whim, I get barred for life.

DeNevi, my supervisor for twelve years, without whose support and encouragement I would have left SQ years ago—even he suddenly throws me under the bus without one phone call, and Don usually calls several times a week and has from the beginning. Am I developing a paranoid frame of mind? Maybe.

36

Letter of Resignation

May 27, 2012

Dear Don,

Without your support I would have left the baseball program at San Quentin years ago. Now in what would have been my 17th season, I must resign from the program. And without you, there would not have been the incredibly great sports programs enjoyed at the prison. Thank you for all you have done.

Let me express why I am leaving. One, in 2010 we decided, at the close of that season, to add one team—the A's. After contacting the Oakland A's, they supplied us with uniforms, and we were off and running. I invited a particular coach to manage the A's, but he consistently, and again this 2012 season, essentially turned it over to a convict to run. Yes, two other coaches that I brought in to work with the A's in 2011 ran into some significant trouble, resulting in a player being transferred to another institution, but that 2011 season, due to the problem coaches and the inattention of the manager of the A's, resulted in a miserable season for all concerned. The rivalry and tension was suffocating at times, and few felt good about the season.

I was forced out of the prison in late July of 2011 because of threats floated against me. The most interesting accusation against me was "reverse" racism, due to the fact that a high percentage of the Giants were black; the "white boys" on the A's did not appreciate this.

In a later meeting with the CDW, Chief Deputy Warden, I was assured that the problem was taken care of, but it was not; it got worse.

Also, for 2012, we made format changes designed to correct the problems from the previous season, but as it turned out, that plan failed. Then more threats were made against me and one other coach, meetings were held in the CDW's office, where I had to endure what could only be described as a "thug/bully" talking to, without even one sentence spoken by me or a moment when I was given a chance to speak. This occurred not once but three times, at each of which you were present. After the Investigative Unit finished their report, I was removed from the prison along with the two problem A's coaches. At no time, despite my thirty years of volunteer work at the prison, was I ever personally interviewed, except for a brief telephone conversation. I have never had a chance to even ask what it was that I was being punished for.

At a meeting with the chief people running the two baseball teams on May 25, I was pressured into allowing certain problem people, three of whom had been involved with the problem mentioned above, to remain in the baseball program. (At least one of these should have been transferred to another prison.) And then, on Saturday, May 26, when the names of those selected for the A's and the Giant's were read off, the problem coach for the A's handed the job of running the team to the convict who was behind so much of the mischief.

This last reason was enough for me. The program was not safe for anyone; the convicts were running the A's team once again.

Then, on May 27, I received a letter of resignation from the one coach without whom the program could not go on. He was the co-manager of the Giants and my good friend, who, citing safety concerns, decided enough was enough.

Here is the bottom line on this sad affair: The CDW so managed the situation that the baseball program was made unsafe. Don, you did your best to dissuade him, but due to his "thug/bully" means of dealing with prison staff and volunteers, there was little you could do.

Below is a copy of the email I sent out to the managers of the teams so far scheduled to come into the prison in 2012. It was my duty to let them know this. There were virtually no coaches left to run two teams, two practices a week, and two games against outside teams per week. There was no other choice.

Hello Everyone,

A sad time for me and for you and your players: there will be no season at the prison this year. I am hoping that, after the dust settles, that we will have a 2013 season. Let me tell you in a greatly abbreviated form, however, what brought us to this point.

One, considerable trouble among our coaches. (How's that for brief?)

Two, utterly unsafe conditions. Some months ago, West Block went general population, that is, mainline prisoners, 800 plus of them, occupied the block. Due to budget concerns, these Level 3 convicts, by the stroke of an administration pen, became Level 2. This meant they were all eligible to come down on the yard and participate in the sports programs. My first sight of them was when I went with my son Vernon, who runs the flag football program, to observe two games. One look and I could see that everything had changed. Young, aggressive, three race groups, white (looked like the Hell's Angel's rejects due to being too rowdy), blacks, and Hispanics, all ganged up and looking to figure out who was going to call the shots, deal the dope, and control some rather unsavory realities of prison life.

I cannot, after what has happened in the last few days, justify inviting anyone into the prison right now. There will be those who will disagree with me, but I have to act according to my conscience. I have done the inviting and the scheduling, so the burden is on me. I am aware that there would be those who would push for the season to move along anyway, but it is my view that this is not only impossible but dangerous. The final decision was made clear to me this morning when I got a letter of resignation from the coach I have been working with for years. We actually have coached the Giants together for the last two years, and he cited safety concerns.

So, there we are. Perhaps there will be a 2013 season, but things have to shake out so we can see what kind of adjustments are made. Word I have is that it takes a year or so before the hierarchy is established and the pecking order made plain.

Thank you for being willing to come in and play our guys.
Kent Philpott

Don, I am sorry it came to this. You did you best, and none of this is any fault of your own. When the program came under the purview of the CDW, for whatever reasons, he micro-managed it to its demise. All the promises he made to make things safe on the lower yard not only did not work but made things worse. Now my son to a lesser degree, but I for sure, have to be concerned about what it might mean to have a prison gang thinking who knows what.

On my wall are a couple photos of you and I on the yard at opening days. I will not forget you. Thank you for all you did.
Kent Philpott

37

Back In: Six Years Later

Tomorrow, Saturday, May 26, 2018, I go back into the prison. To catch up a little, I will relate part of my history there.

For the first four years, 1997 to 2000, Dan Jones and I managed the San Quentin Pirates/Giants. Dan had to leave due to medical issues. I continued alone for a number of years with a couple of guys I brought in to lighten the load. Then about 2009 several baseball guys came in to serve as real coaches. Chief of these is Kevin Laughlin, whom I met when our two teams (the Tamalpais Hawks frosh team and Kevin's frosh team, the San Rafael Bulldogs) played each other at Albert's Park in San Rafael, 2005. (This is the field where the Pacifics now play.)

Besides Kevin, there were several other coaches. One of them showed up occasionally, mostly Saturday mornings; he would arrive late and leave early. His main focus was criticizing the operation. After I left, during 2012, Kevin managed the team up until he was also forced to leave.

Son Vernon was also kicked out a few months later. Vern had taken over the Blues Brothers, an 8-man flag football team I had begun some years earlier. Being a Philpott, he had to go.

Then one of the other coaches, a real baseball guy, solid coach, faithful, had a home invasion take place and was shot but survived. It was a message sent from the **********. He concealed all this from the prison officials and came back in the next season, I think 2014. Parcels would arrive at his house with instructions to take the baseball equipment—baseball gloves mostly—into the prison in his equipment bag. All he had to do was, whenever the A's played or practiced, leave the bag in the A's dugout on the first base line. Simple as that.

Finding that you could stuff about 1,000-plus meth tablets into a hollowed-out catcher's mitt, he called son Vernon on the phone. Vern visited this man's new residence and took photos of the contraband. This was the last straw, and this coach never went back in, destroyed the dope, and hoped he would not be attacked again.

Back now to the coach who loved to criticize me—in 2013 or 2014—he took over managing the team, except with a difference. He merely acted as a sponsor, bringing outside teams in but leaving the running of practices and games to the convicts. Mistake. This of course worked for the ********** as they could continue in various ingenious ways to get drugs and cell phones into the prison. And one particular gang did this—what we call "The White Boys."

Yes, there are gangs in San Quentin, but all under cover, almost. If someone is identified as a gang member, they are shipped out to a higher security level prison like Corcoran, High Desert, or Pelican Bay among others. SQ is a level 2 prison, and due to things like the age of the structures, it does not provide the kind of security necessary.

Nevertheless, controlling drugs is power, and the cell phones allow gangs to do all kinds of wonderful things. I could go on and describe what power means in a prison, but I'll forgo that for now.

This baby-sitting coach (Do I sound angry?) ran the program down. Every year attempts were made to get me back in. A number of the inmates, the head of the athletic program, and one other person whom I will not name eventually succeeded in bringing me back in. Somehow this one person was able to convince the Internal Security Unit (ISU) to allow it.

For two or more years I would get a call from the ISU and talk to a sergeant or lieutenant who would say something like, "Look Philpott, I have your file in front of me, and if we were to let you back in and something happened to you, the State of California would be on the hook." My response was always, "I understand."

Tomorrow I will park in the lot below the visitor's center, I plan to get there about 8:20am, wait for a beige card holder, one of the present coaches, and get through the East Gate, make the long walk to the Count Gate, sign in, and walk into the prison past the Catholic, Protestant, Jewish, Muslim, American Indian, and other chapels, turn right at the hospital building, head right down cardiac hill and into the lower year. On the right will be a giant wall with the gun towers situated along it, and the inmates will spot me. On the left is an old iron door, fenced off now, where the old morgue was. When I get down past the "Out of bounds" sign painted on the tarmac, and the cons spot me, who knows what might happen. But I suspect there will be some who will recognize the old coach and come up to meet me with some amount of friendship. We'll see. Because I am bound to see guys I was close to, sometimes for years, it will be quite emotional for me.

Let me state why I am going back in. First, I spent 32 years as a volunteer at San Quentin, 16 of those years as the baseball coach. I was removed because of a gang's need to bring in drugs and cell phones. There was not a goodbye, no thanks, no nothing. I want to go out on my own terms, not due to death threats, finish with my own resignation, after some years. I am seventy-six years old, and I think I still have some good years left. And frankly, coaching at the prison is a whole lot easier than doing high school baseball.

The second reason for going back in is that I want to start a second team, The Pirates. The Pirates, which is the name of the original team and the third generation of baseball at San Quentin, was begun by Chaplin Earl Smith in 1995. The Pirates became the Giants in 1999 when the San Francisco Giants donated uniforms and equipment to us. Chaplain Smith was the SF Giants chaplain, the first African American to be a chaplain in the state's prison system, and he made it work. Earl is, by the way, still the chaplain for the San Francisco 49ers and the Golden State Warriors. Side note: one of his sons, Franklin, I see from time to time, as he is the head coach for the San Rafael Bulldogs Junior Varsity baseball team. I watched Franklin and his brother, Earl Jr., grow up while they lived on the grounds of the prison.

One story I will tell about Earl Jr. Around 2007 I pulled up to get gas at the Chevron Station on Miller Avenue in Mill Valley. The guy pumping gas in front of me was Earl. We shook hands and I asked him, and I am not sure why I did this, but I asked him if he knew how I could get a pair of cleats for a guy with a size 14 shoe. Earl did not say a word, but opened the trunk of his car, reached in, grabbed a pair of brand-new cleats, sized 14, and handed them to me. Typical of the Smith family.

Okay, another story. At a high school game, at home playing the San Rafael Bulldogs, I was standing against the rail at our third base dugout. The game was about to begin when the opposition's coach walked in and took his place at the third base coach's box. A big Black man, full beard and all, and he was looking directly, and hard, at me. In a moment he yelled out, "Philpott!" It was Franklin Smith, Earl's brother and son of Earl Smith. The baseball world in Marin County is a small one.

Tomorrow I am going to attempt to let the guys know of my intention. The baby-sitting coach refused to allow a second team—too much trouble. And he would be right, but I did it for years and want to do it again.

Either there will be another team or there will be another paragraph below saying my plan did not work.

Here's how the visit went. It was a huge success. I was overwhelmed by the response from the guys, many I knew, many I did not know. As I feed this into the computer, I am still having a stunned feeling. The short of it is, they want me back and as soon as possible. The program has been a mess since I left, according to several dozen inmates, and not only the baseball program but the football program as well.

Of course, I do not believe everything that was said to me, but I had four rather long and serious conversations with former players I trust, and I am convinced I heard correctly. My most trusted informant told me that scores of young offenders, ages 18 to 24, are coming into San Quentin, mostly on drug charges, and that there will be 50-plus guys wanting to play for the Pirates. Looks like the 'Skull and Cross Bones' will fly again.

Appendix A

Bill's Story

Here is an account of a game played at San Quentin between the Pirates, now Giants, and the Oaks/Cubs, the very same team led by Elliot Smith that opened the 2010 season. My oldest and dear friend Bill Mauck and his son Michael were present and played in the game. Here is Bill's story of that game.

We Had a Great Time
by Bill Mauck

Thursday, March 13, 1998, was a cold, cloudy day at San Quentin penitentiary. As my nineteen-year-old son, Michael, and I approached the front gate, I could feel a light drizzle against my face. We were greeted by a guard. He checked our names off the manifest, wanded us down and checked our gear. We walked about 200 yards to the main prison walls, where another guard repeated the same process. We were then directed through a series of electronically controlled steel doors. As the last door slammed behind us, we emerged into a vast courtyard. The mood became dark, almost surreal. To our right were some gray buildings. One of the buildings had the words "Attitude Adjustment Center" etched on the wall. Instinctively I knew we did not want to go there. To my right were some men in bright orange jumpsuits. I later learned these men were HIV positive.

At the far end of the courtyard was a baseball diamond. As I walked out onto the infield, I could smell the fresh cut grass. I felt my cleats dig into the soft turf. It felt good! It had been a while. My high school friend, Kent Philpott, is a minister in Mill Valley, and he coaches the San Quentin Pirates baseball team.

As it turns out, the Pirates were scheduled to play the San Francisco Oaks Semi-pro baseball team this day, and the Oaks were going to be short a couple of players. Kent invited Mike and me to come down for a visit and play in this game.

While Mike and I were warming up with the other players along the right field line, the Oaks coach observed us and made some quick decisions. It was determined that Mike would lead off and play second base. I would bat ninth and be dispatched to right field. Right field is unique at San Quentin. There is only about two feet of grass in foul territory along the right field foul line. It then becomes a concrete slab. Right field is short, only about 290 feet to the warning track. Normally the warning track is dirt. Outfielders can feel their cleats dig into the dirt when they come off the grass and this lets them know they are about ten feet from the fence. At San Quentin the warning track is asphalt. After the warning track the surface becomes concrete. There is no fence; instead, there are benches and tables. This is special, as it makes it possible for the inmates to sit, enjoy the game and make helpful suggestions to the opposing team's right fielder.

In right center field is the Indian Nation. The Indians have some tepees, sweat-houses, drums and there are fires burning. The nation is protected by a forty-foot-tall portable handmade screen made of woven cloth and called the White Monster. The Native Americans' religion says that you can sweat your sins away.

So here I am, a fifty-eight-year-old man taking my position in right field. Off my right shoulder, I can hear the tom-toms. Thump thump, thump thump, thump thump. My nostrils fill with smoke. My eyes are burning. Off my left shoulder, I can hear the constant chatter of the prisoners. "Hey, Col. Sanders, Mon! How 'bout some chicken wings and cerveza for the homeboys in right field." "Hey, Mon! Pops don't have no beer, just look at him. He drank it all up already." Haaaaaaa, I started thinking to myself. Self, you are a first baseman. What the hell are you doing in right field?! Then I thought maybe I'll get lucky, and nothing will get hit out here. Baseball has an old and true axiom. It states that the ball will find you. It didn't take long. In the first inning the Pirates hit three hard ground balls in my direction. I was able to get in front of the ball and hit the cutoff man. Everything was all good until this big left-handed hitter came up and hit a high fly ball to straightaway right field. I raced back. I felt my cleats dig into the asphalt and then clank on the concrete. I looked down. The inmates scattered. I weaved my way through the benches, but when I looked back up, I had lost the flight of the ball. The ball landed on a table and caromed off a bench. Buy the time I retrieved the ball the runner had rounded third base and was on his way home. Things did not get better. Next, they started hitting balls over on to the concrete in foul territory. Cleats have a tendency to slip and slide on concrete. I didn't catch any of them. I walked and struck out. I began to think that I had swerved into the twilight zone of baseball.

My son, Mike, did much better. He struck the ball hard and made some good plays in the field. When Mike steps into the batter's box he assumes an open stance, with his feet set about three feet apart. As he stands in, he likes to move his hips from side to side. This drew some interesting comments from some of the more progressive inmates. The San Quentin Pirates had a good team; they beat the Oaks eight to two. After the game the mood was jovial, we shook hands and exchanged pleasantries. Had this game been played anywhere else, I would not have guessed that these men were convicts.

We returned to my friend's home. We sat in Kent's arbor and enjoyed a cold bottle of beer. I began to lament about some of my play. Kent philosophized that baseball would keep me humble. Mike spoke up and said, "Chill, Dad! You gave it your best shot. I had a great time." I looked at my son and realized that this was one of those defining moments. We had played this game not as father and son, but as just two players. It was a day that each of us would remember. I looked at him and replied, "You are right, Mike. I had a great time too."

Appendix B

Doug's Story

Going Yard
by Doug McKenzie

"When we go into the prison, you'll definitely feel some anxiety." The prophecy came from Bob, our manager for the doubleheader against the San Quentin inmate baseball team, when I'd first contacted him two months prior to joining his squad.

I knew he was right. But I decided to get an early start and let the anxiety build as soon as I committed to play.

Two months is a long time to let my imagination work. Much too long.

As expected, visions of being cornered in the yard after getting separated from the group worked their way into my head. Of somehow ticking-off the wrong guy on the opposing team. Of ending up on the wrong end of the shiv that the first baseman snuck into the game.

One link bound them all—I returned home maimed or worse in each one.

I'd heard the warnings. Once we hit the yard, we'd be subjected to a wave of trash talk and thrown expletives. I didn't even know the proper prison protocol for a visitor. Smack talk back? It might get me some respect. Or it might lead directly to one of those visions.

But another part of me longed for the experience. The part that doesn't miss a prison exposé on cable. The part that wants to hear that iron gate close behind me. To feel the starkness of the yard. To see if the walls really do close in. To be in the world of some guy who chopped his best friend into 107 pieces and then buried him in 107 different places.

I wanted to experience that world—live it—for just for a little while. And I love baseball. What better way to accomplish it than combine the two?

My M.O. isn't hard to predict. I knew the anxiety would peak the night before the game. It'd be hard to sleep. Probably wouldn't have any appetite in the morning.

Then I got a lucky break.

Justin, from my amateur team back home, had signed up to play as well.

A few years transplanted from Australia, Justin's a natural athlete. He picked up baseball as easy as my dog picked up begging at the table. It's impossible to get a low-pitch by him. Must be from all those years of cricket.

Far more important for this adventure, he's about as easygoing a guy as you can find. It's tough to get him upset. I've tried. Everyone on my team has tried.

We chatted in the hotel about what the next day might bring, and it turned out he'd visited a maximum-security prison in Australia for a college thesis. The whole thing was no big deal. I half-expected him to fall asleep in the hotel patio as he described it.

Perfect. I was with a vet. My nerves could relax.

That's when he mentioned that they'd probably make us sign a "no negotiations" waiver in case we were taken hostage.

Hostage? It turned out there was one scenario I'd neglected to worry about. Still, I managed to remain calm.

Then I met Kent.

Kent wasn't one of the prisoners—he was their coach. That's on the inside. On the outside, Kent's a pastor. We met him in a weary parking lot outside the gates at 8:30 in the morning where he gave us a quick talk about what to expect. Kent's another easygoing guy—especially for someone about to walk us into a maximum-security prison.

It's what he said that got the nerves working again.

San Quentin's the only prison in the United States that has a baseball team for its inmates. In fact, the program is so popular it's now home to two teams, the Giants and the Pirates. Usually comprised of players from adult amateur leagues, outside teams (known as "The Willing") routinely play a doubleheader at "the Q"—one game against the Giants and one against the Pirates.

Today we'd take on the San Quentin Giants in both games.

The Pirates weren't too happy about this.

Kent said he wasn't sure what to expect. There'd been a lot of unrest at the prison lately. Overcrowding at Corcoran and Pelican Bay had forced the state to send much of the hard-core overflow here. New, young guys had arrived. Lifers who had nothing to lose.

Things weren't the same.

Maybe Kent noticed the widened eyes because he told us not to worry. Nothing would ever happen to a visitor—every prison program in the state would end in a flash.

Kent finished with an admonition: if any of the players from the other team approached us during the game wanting personal information, don't give it to them.

Approached us? From the unhappy team? I thought these were the guys that had nothing to lose.

My carefully administered self-hypnosis—two months in the making—of why I would survive this impending experience shattered. I'd already convinced myself we'd be hermitically sealed with at least three fences and a wall of armed guards partitioning us from anyone that wasn't in the game.

I looked at the veterans of our team—none of whom I'd ever met—to reassure myself, to see the calm look on their faces. Once I saw that "look"—the one people have when they've heard the whole speech before and are bored stiff—I'd be fine.

Instead apprehensive stares filled the audience. My eyes darted to Justin, my last hope. Even he looked slightly concerned. With Justin, that's the equivalent of a panic attack.

The information processing in my head began to blur. New, hard-core guys. Nothing to lose. Trouble. Waivers if I'm taken hostage.

Maybe my friends are right. Maybe I am a masochist. It's a death wish or something. Psychologists would have a field day with me.

One of the new guys broke in, "Just how good a shot are the guards in the tower?" At least someone else was thinking along the same lines as me.

We showed our I.D.s at an outer gate and made the long walk to the prison walls. To our right sat a row of quaint administration buildings. To our left, the rippling currents of the bay reached out forever as if no prison existed. But I took little notice on the gorgeous Saturday morning. Instead a question revolved in my head that my brain couldn't solve… "If the new guys in here have nothing to lose, why would they care if the programs shut down because they did something to a visitor?"

If you've watched any prison documentaries on TV, you know what I expected. I expected the gate to clank behind us and then to be surrounded by my new world, a bleak world of rusted metal and chipped paint, curses shouted at me by every person in view. Undecipherable screams would evaporate into the bay breeze from wherever they kept the people that had gone nuts… or had completely given up hope.

That's what I expected for a prison built in 1852.

My first view gave me exactly the opposite.

A neatly tended courtyard greeted us when we exited the Sallyport (the controlled area between two metal gates), complete with lawn and roses. On the far end, a massive state-of-the-art medical facility dominated the other buildings in the area.

Heading toward the 5-story building, I felt faces peering from barred windows in the archaic building to our left. That building, the kind I'd expected to see, turned out to be the Adjustment Center, a housing unit for the most dangerous inmates on Death Row.

After crossing the courtyard, a long asphalt driveway led us between the new complex now to our left and the ancient wall that separated us from the free world on the right.

The San Quentin yard opened up.

The field wasn't hard to spot—it was the only grass area in an expanse of asphalt, walls and fences. Like a grammar school playground at lunchtime, a flurry of activity surrounded the diamond and filled the yard. Men jockeyed for position as a shot went up on the basketball court. Tennis balls volleyed. And countless guys in dark blue sweats or shorts with light blue shirts just hung around.

But as opposed to my elementary school, a chain link fence didn't surround this yard. Razor wire saturated these surroundings, everywhere, blocking anything anyone could ever think of climbing, crawling or hopping over.

A four-foot space between two chain link fences would serve as our dugout. Inside the partition, it took me a few minutes to realize that the long metal thing that looked like a narrow table was actually our bench.

The home team took the field. I'd expected them to be in prison garb, but they had full uniforms (courtesy of the major league team), with an orange "Giants" emblazoned across black jerseys. Their roster would be a few short today; anybody residing in H-block was absent. A few prisoners in that unit had contracted a virus. As a result, the whole block locked-down, a precaution due to the speed an epidemic can spread in a closed-off prison.

Beyond the clover outfield, the warning track contoured around the ins and outs of the fences that bordered our field. The difference between this field and any other where I've played quickly struck me. The spectators were inside the fences. Prisoners lined the edges of the field, some in cliques, some loners, while many others walked or jogged the "warning track" that looped the yard.

A new concern surfaced, hidden in the back of my mind by the question as to whether I'd survive the visit. Was I even good enough to play in this game? I'm 50 and live for baseball. Sundays are dedicated to amateur ball in the 35 and older division of the Los Angeles Baseball League. In that league, most have played long enough to have success because of our fundamentals. But the arms are starting to go (if they're not gone already). The bat slows down. The reflexes. Though I do well, I no longer face 20-year old hurlers—the pitchers that can bring it.

Right away I saw their starter brought a hot fastball. Just what I didn't need.

We'd bat "through," a common practice in adult amateur baseball where everyone on a 12 to 14 man roster bats instead of a traditional nine-man line-up. It gives everyone a shot to participate. Free defensive substitution is also allowed as opposed to more formal baseball rules.

We pushed across an unearned run in the first, but the Giants countered with a pair in the bottom of the inning. Defense was sloppy; maybe I wasn't the only one who was feeling the nerves.

The pebbles that saturated the all-dirt infield didn't build confidence fielding the ground balls hit to me at second. Still, the prisoners had obviously worked hard to make the field the best possible. Not easy to do because, as Kent said, tools equal potential weapons.

By the time I first came to the plate in the second I was sure of one thing. Stay off the high fastball. Their pitcher had too much heat for me—I'd never get around on it.

Our games on Sunday don't have big crowds. A few of the guys' wives show up with the kids. Maybe someone's girlfriend. That's about it. I played at a small college, and the attendance there wasn't any bigger.

In the yard, I was in front of the biggest crowd of my life. The quintessential captive audience. But no catcalls or trash talk filled the air as I expected. It didn't matter. I still felt the pressure. As any athlete will admit, you want to go in and show the guys—on both squads—that you can play, that you're not some slug that tagged along and drags the team down. That you're not that kid we all remember in the Pee-wee leagues—the last one picked—the one that swung after the ball was in the catcher's glove. I didn't want to be that kid.

Not here.

I take a high fastball that catches the corner. The home plate ump, Junkyard (who has by far the coolest name of any umpire I've ever taken the field with) calls strike one. Another fastball—up. I swing. Late. Down oh and two.

Stay off that pitch. Poke something somewhere. Whatever you do, don't "K" to start this day off.

Not here.

Fastball, low and away. I take it.

Junkyard rings me up. Three pitches. This day couldn't have started worse. Back to the metal table-looking thing.

A 3D puzzle of dilapidated structures sits beyond left-center. Archaic stairs lead up and down the sides of faded yellow walls then turn to mysterious passageways before disappearing into areas unknown. But my eyes fix past the maze of buildings to the notorious housing unit, West Block that looms above them. A plume of steam pours out from one of the puzzle pieces to obscure the view. It's like a Dickens novel that's come to life.

The prisoners responsible for hanging the numbers on the "Field of Dreams" scoreboard in right don't dally after each half inning. And they don't give the benefit of the doubt on errors—even for the home club—as the miscues total almost as much as the score.

After six, we're deadlocked at five. But Kent has a wedding to perform between games, so it'll be a shortened contest. No inning will start later than 12:30.

It's 12:20 now. The seventh is it.

That doesn't bode well for us. The SQ starter threw well, but the Giants now have Stretch on the mound to close it out. The tall and lanky righty is likely San Quentin's most famous player because he's so good.

Stretch doesn't throw as hard as their starter, but he quickly shows why he's earned the reputation as a stellar pitcher. It's not his wide array of pitches; it's his great command of them. You're not going to get anything good.

A hit, a stolen base and an out manages to move our go ahead runner to third.

It's our last chance. And guess who's coming up for us…

I'm oh for two at this point. In baseball, ohfers are long forgotten if you knock in the winning run. All game I've been eyeing the short porch in right like the lifer who's spotted a hole in the wall. There's some sort of caged-off material yard that shortens the field there. Any batted-ball that makes the top of the cage is a homer. It can't be more than a 280-foot poke. Probably shorter. In my Sunday league, I'll pop one out about once every two seasons with a metal bat. But this I can reach, even with the wood we're using.

Stretch makes his only mistake all day—he leaves one out over the plate. Slightly outside. I couldn't ask for a better pitch to go the other way.

Excitement raced through my veins as I ran to first. I didn't think I'd hit it well enough to make the top of the cage, but it certainly would be off the fence. I'd return home to tell everyone about my game winning shot at San Quentin.

That's when I learned a new aspect of playing in the yard. Baseballs don't carry as well above the wall as they do below it.

My liner had taken off like a rocket, but once it got above the level of the wall, it died in the bay breeze like it'd been shot by a guard while trying to escape. Not only didn't it make the fence, it didn't even make the track with the walking prisoners. I watched it die, futilely dropping to the right fielder who was playing shallow by necessity of the short field. My "blast" succumbed so quickly I wasn't even sure it'd score the guy on third.

But in his eagerness to nail our guy at home, the right fielder misplayed the ball. The go-ahead scored. As far as I was concerned—as far as the legend would go—I'd crushed the game-winning RBI sac fly off San Quentin's star pitcher. No official scorekeeper would contradict me later.

The Giants launched a furious rally in the bottom of the inning, but couldn't score. We'd taken Game One. From ohfer to hero at San Quentin.

Wait…

The Giants wanted to continue. They weren't going to lose this game. Not by one run. Coach Kent could go marry the couple. They'd go on without him.

Despite the fact that my game-hero status was likely doomed, I had a begrudging admiration for the Giants' insistence to go on. It was like when you were a kid and stalled when it was time to go in for dinner because you wanted to keep playing outside.

We couldn't touch Stretch after that. But we still thought we had it until we gave up one (almost two) in the bottom of the ninth. A tie. And my game-winning "shot" turned into kiss your sister.

We did the congratulation line, with hugs. I wasn't worried about shivs anymore. Stretch led both teams in prayer. They thanked us for coming to play. I couldn't remember receiving more genuine gratitude.

Despite the whispered rumors in the dugout during the game, "three quarters of them are in for murder," I never bothered to find out what each guy was in for. I didn't really care. On this day, they weren't any different from us. They were just guys out playing ball.

Our team packed up our gear and started back toward the driveway. Lunch would be outside the prison. I lagged a bit at the bench to undo my knee-brace. The anxiety was long gone.

That's when the prison alarm went off.

Instantly every inmate dropped to a squat. Except for the loud drone of the buzzer, there wasn't a movement or sound in the yard.

I'd almost forgotten where I was.

I didn't know what to do. The team huddled 100 feet away. I heard a voice from somewhere say not to worry about it. I think it was directed to us, but I didn't know what that meant. Should I make a move to get back with my group? If I bolted for them I'd be the only moving person in the yard. Now wasn't the time to find out how good a shot the guards in the towers really were.

After a few minutes, the buzzer stopped and I hustled to the group. I would hear it three more times in the second game.

We'd win that one going away—our pitcher brought his good stuff on a late Saturday afternoon. It was already well past seven when we said our goodbyes in the parking lot. I drove off, wondering what I'd ever been so anxious about.

As I hopped on the freeway, a small insignificant sign I'd seen posted on the fence behind first base reappeared in my head. "FEEDING PIGEONS WILL RESULT IN CDC #115 BEING ISSUED."

I didn't have a clue what a CDC #115 meant other than the prisoners obviously would want to avoid getting it. In our outside world, that sign would have no meaning. Instead it would read something like, "$100 fine for feeding pigeons."

Theirs was a world where they knew what that CDC code meant. And what every other CDC code meant, complete with its potential consequences.

A world where they knew what to do when the buzzer went off in the yard.

I'd come to try to live their world for a few brief hours and then be able to run back home where I'd be safe. But there really was only so much I could experience as a visitor. I could feel the flavor, but not know what it was to live the life.

Instead I was rewarded with an experience that I'd taken for granted the entire adventure. I'd joined a bunch of guys, from both sides of the wall, and for a day shared the same game we both loved.

And I drove off, looking forward to playing them again next year.

Douglas Y. MacKenzie
Glendale, CA

www.ingramcontent.com/pod-product-compliance
Lightning Source LLC
Chambersburg PA
CBHW061150070526
44584CB00034B/4470